REAL-LIFE *Cinderella*

THE STORY OF *Brandy*

REAL-LIFE

Cinderella

THE STORY OF

Brandy

BY JOAL RYAN

BALLANTINE BOOKS

THE BALLANTINE PUBLISHING GROUP • NEW YORK

W

This is an independent biographical work and is not authorized in any way by
Brandy Norwood.

A Ballantine Book
Published by The Ballantine Publishing Group

Copyright © 1998 by Byron Preiss Visual Publications, Inc.

www.randomhouse.com/BB/

Library of Congress Cataloging-in-Publication Data
Ryan, Joal.
Real-life cinderella: the story of brandy/Joal Ryan—1st ed.
p.   cm.
Includes
ISBN 0-345-43375-0

Edited by Steven Roman
Cover and interior design by Gilda Hannah

Cover photograph of Brandy
Copyright © 1996 Fitzroy Barrett/Globe Photos, Inc.

Page 1 photograph of Brandy
Copyright © 1998 Andrea Renault/Globe Photos, Inc.

Page 2 photographs of Brandy
Copyright © 1995 Walter Weissman/Globe Photos, Inc.,
and Copyright © 1996 Lisa Rose/Globe Photos, Inc.

Page 6 photograph of Brandy
Copyright © 1998 Fitzroy Barrett/Globe Photos, Inc.

Pages 8-9 spread photograph of the cast of *Moesha*
Copyright © 1996 Andrea Renault/Globe Photos, Inc.

Manufactured in the United States of America

First Edition: December 1998

10 9 8 7 6 5 4 3 2 1

For Kurt Vonnegut

Thanks to: Dennis Bent, Herbert Byrd, John & Alice Ryan,
Steve Ryfle, Art Warp, and Spark Dogg.

Special thanks to: Steve Roman, Peter Rubie,
and Elizabeth Zack and Jason Zuzga at Ballantine Books.

contents

"From the second I laid eyes
on her, I knew she was
going to be a superstar."

RON SHAPIRO
Atlantic Record's
executive vice-president
and general manager

chapter one **never say never**

> "She *is* Cinderella."
> —Whitney Houston

With apologies to Ms. Houston, no, she's *not*. She's Brandy. And that's more than enough.

Maybe even better.

Cinderella, you see, is a make-believe princess. Brandy is a real-live superstar— with the best-selling CDs, the style-setting TV show, the burgeoning film career, and the fashion-dictating magazine covers to prove it.

As for Cindy? A lousy pair of uncomfy, unsuitable-for-winter-wear glass slippers—tops.

So, we clear on this? The name's Brandy. She's got it going on all four burners. And she won't be twenty-one until the built-for-the-future twenty-first century is a couple months old.

This is her story.

So far.

So long.

So cool.

dreams

Preceding spread: Brandy makes an enchanting entrance in Rodgers & Hammerstein's Cinderella. *(Copyright © 1997 ABC-TV. Supplied by Photofest.)*

Opposite: Brandy at rehearsals for a City Kids Foundation program. (Copyright © 1995 Andrea Renault/Globe Photos, Inc.)

Inset: Brandy with her mother, Sonja Norwood, at the premiere of Cinderella. (Copyright © 1997 Fitzroy Barrett/Globe Photos, Inc.)

"A lot of times I look at my life," Brandy once told the *Mr. Showbiz* Web site, "and I just feel like it's a dream."

What was the giveaway? The Top 10 hit ("I Wanna Be Down") at age fifteen? The No. 1 hit ("The Boy Is Mine" with Monica) at age nineteen? The night back in 1997 when sixty million people watched her play Cinderella in the ABC-TV musical? The all-star friendships and collaborations (with Mase, Monica, Usher, Whitney Houston, Boyz II Men)? The chance to segue into film stardom in the eagerly awaited horror flick *I Still Know What You Did Last Summer*?

No matter. The first thing, you see, to know about Brandy Rayana Norwood is that this—career, life, stardom—is *not* a dream.

No, not even the prom date with the top-round NBA draft pick. Sure, maybe if you're the leading lady of Generation Next and you're doing an inventory of credits—the chart busters ("Brokenhearted," "Baby"), the mega-rated TV special (*Rodgers & Hammerstein's Cinderella*), the long-running TV series (*Moesha*), the runway fashion shows in Milan—you're entitled to pinch yourself. ("Sometimes I wish somebody would pinch me," Brandy said to *Vibe* magazine.) But fact is, it's *not* a dream.

The second thing to know is Brandy *is* a dream, or pretty close to it. A clean-talking, clean-living holdout in the era of the toxic celebrity. Chafe as she may at her persona as the Virginal Good Girl of Pop Music ("I'm human," she has pleaded, as if to try to convince us of her mere mortal status), she doesn't go out of her way to tarnish the tiara, either. No rowdy nightclubbing. No tattoo flaunting. No police-blotter courting. To be sure, she is growing—as an artist, as a person. ("I'm nineteen! If I want to have sex, I have every right to," she told *Seventeen*.) But she also is what she is: a young adult who, despite a far-flung career, still bunks at Camp Mom and Dad. Write it off as an "act" (and Brandy knows some do) or accept it as the real deal, it's still a dream. A welcome one.

The third—and perhaps key—thing to know is Brandy is, like we said, *not* Cinderella. Even if she donned glass slippers before

a nationwide television audience. Even if her superstar mentor and friend Whitney Houston insists otherwise. Even if her life to date suggests the trappings of a fairy tale. But despite evidence to the contrary, the realities of being a touched-by-magic princess are a bit much even for Brandy's capable self. To be Cinderella is to be unreal, unblemished, and—face it—real lucky.

The bottom line is, you don't get to be Brandy, don't get to move in Brandy's smooth circles, don't get to do the stuff Brandy does on a free pass from a fairy godmother.

You get there by doing. (Singing in Dad's church choir, singing to anyone or anything with ears.) By being clear about what you want. (No sleep till you're on Whitney's career track.) By being brave and bold and crazy enough to take the leap. (World-class celebritydom? Sure, why not?) And by being flat-out strong enough to stick the landing.

Brandy put a beat to this philosophy. It's called "Never Say Never." The title cut of her second album is ostensibly a love song—a couple's defiant "we're still here" pose—but it is more effectively a theme song. Brandy's theme song.

The goal of Miss Norwood's "Never Say Never" attitude, obviously, was to become an A-list entertainer. But the MO pretty much works for would-be doctors, movie directors, or deep-sea divers, too.

As Brandy wrote in the liner notes to her self-titled 1994 debut album: "Whatever your dreams are, you, too, can make them come true."

Deep? Profound? That's debatable. (Hey, she was *fifteen*.) But not easily dismissed, either. After all, if there's one thing Brandy Norwood is an expert on, it's dreams.

beginnings

The first dream was dreamed by Sonja Norwood.

It was February 11, 1979, in McComb, Mississippi, a small (population: 13,000, circa 1990), mostly agricultural town with modest, if sturdy, credentials: one high school, one mall, lots of churches. Up until then, McComb was best known in modern-day music annals for two things: serving as the birth place of Rock and Roll Hall of Famer Bo Diddley ("Who Do You Love?"), and being the touring-plane crash site of Lynyrd Skynyrd, the long-haired, Southern-fried, 1970s rock band ("Free Bird").

Then came February 11, 1979. Sonja, pregnant with her and husband Willie's first child, went into labor.

Now, women under the influence of childbirth are prone to say all sorts of semicoherent and incoherent things—a throaty

Brandy steps out with her parents, Sonja and Willie Ray Norwood, Sr. (Copyright © 1998 Milan Ryba/Globe Photos, Inc.)

"Ow!" being chief among them. But Sonja, a financial analyst by trade, kept her keen head. She sized up the situation, sized up her newborn, and, perhaps in a combination of hunch and determination, informed the doctor that her babe—all of a couple minutes old—was going to be something. Really something.

"I told the doctor he had just delivered a star," Sonja told *People* magazine.

This designated future star, born under the sign of Aquarius, the do-gooding Water Bearer, was named Brandy Rayana.

From the moment she was bundled into her first pair of diapers, the little girl was on the fast track. A solid family background can score you that sort of lane assignment. First off, she had her mom—a woman who saw stars in the delivery room, and, most important, a woman who learned the art of turning dreams into reality from her own father, successful McComb businessman Freddie ("Paw Paw") Bates. And equally first off, she had her dad, Willie Ray Norwood, Sr., a man with the gifts of faith and music.

"My father taught me everything I know," Brandy intoned in the intro to her tribute-paying groove, "I Dedicate."

What Willie knew, among other things, was gospel music. He was a church choral director. His most famous student would become his own daughter.

Before she could talk, Brandy sang. It soon became fairly obvious what Mom's predicted star would become a star at doing: Brandy sang to her family, she sang to her toys, she just plain *sang*.

"When Brandy woke up in the morning, she was singing," Willie told *Vibe*.

The Norwood house in McComb was filled with the byproducts of this melody making. In addition to Brandy's fledgling stabs at vocals, there was dad Willie (by all accounts, a strong singer in his own right), lullaby-cooing grandparents, and, starting in 1981, a younger sibling, Willie Ray Norwood, Jr. Later known as the aspiring actor and R&B star Ray J, little brother got a quick read on how things worked at the Norwoods.

"I always heard my sister and my dad sing," Ray J said in *People*.

Brandy and her brother, Ray J, at the premiere of Set It Off. *(Copyright © 1996 Fitzroy Barrett/Globe Photos, Inc.)*

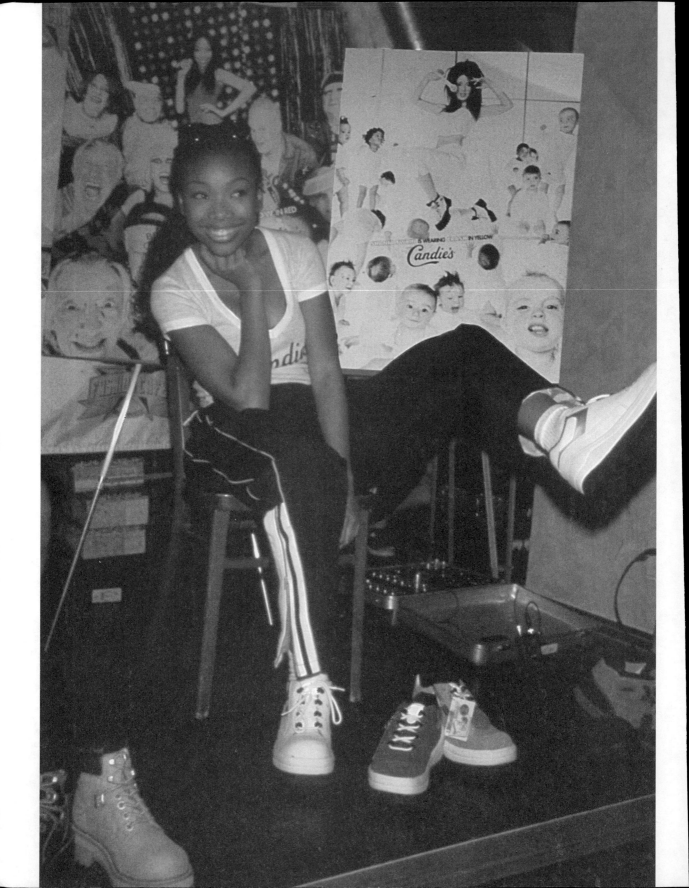

It was at age two, in fact, that Brandy made her concert debut: a solo performance of the gospel staple "Jesus Loves Me" for an audience of churchgoers at a congregation in neighboring Brookhaven, Mississippi. The performance, in keeping with the tenets of the Church of Christ, was rendered a cappella. No backing music. No smoke. Certainly no mirrors. Just Brandy's voice.

It was enough.

And then at age four, the announcement. Brandy told her father that she wanted to be a singer. No smoke. No mirrors. No tap dancing. Just a flat-out "I want to be a singer."

You gotta love a kid with a plan.

With all this energy, with all this bubbling ambition, it wasn't long before the whole family was ready to bust out. McComb is a fine place—hometown of Bo Diddley (remember?), the scene of key civil rights–era struggles, and a safe and sane neighborhood to raise a kid—but it's still *McComb*. An hour and a half away from the nearest big city, New Orleans, and seemingly a million miles away from music-scene meccas like New York or Nashville or Seattle or Detroit. Or Los Angeles.

Geography was no small consideration to Sonja and Willie. They looked at their preschoolers and saw preternatural talent and disposition. To the Norwoods, Los Angeles would not only offer easier access to major record labels, it would offer entrée into its illustrious moviedom cousin, Hollywood.

Thing of it was, Sonja was still the trained numbers cruncher; Willie, the choir director. Admirable professions both, but as far as shark-infested show business went? They would be perceived as novices. Bloodless Hollywood players would relish the chance to carve them up.

But the Norwoods didn't—and don't—scare easily.

"I can sell my kids," confident Sonja once told *Vibe* during a Brandy photo shoot near the Pacific Ocean. "I can sell my kids to the ocean, and the ocean would buy them."

And so in 1983, the same year Brandy declared her professional ambitions, Sonja and Willie packed it in in their native McComb and headed west. To see if the ocean was buying.

To see if dreams worth dreaming were worth living.

Brandy strikes a pose for a new Candie's shoe ad campaign. (Copyright © 1998 Andrea Renault/Globe Photos, Inc.)

chapter two learn the hard way

> "You have to stick your neck
> out and do things."
>
> — Brandy

The latter-day pioneer spirit took the Norwoods to Carson, California, a racially mixed working-class community (population 84,000, circa 1990) that, in the urban, social sprawl that is Southern California, fits somewhere between the gangsta-rap home of South Central Los Angeles and Disneyland (and lots of other points in between).

In strict geographic terms, Carson is closer to Hollywood than McComb, Mississippi, but it's *not* Hollywood (even if Whitney Houston's *Waiting to Exhale* director, actor Forest Whitaker, did make a home there for many years). Carson is located in what's known as the South Bay.

In practical terms, the city is in the middle of nowhere. Suffice it to say there aren't any characters from *Beverly Hills 90210* hailing from the South Bay.

So, Brandy and family weren't going to impress anybody with their zip code—

so what? Beverly Hills might look fancy on an address label, but that alone didn't ensure success. Talent and hard work—*they* were the deal breakers. And the Norwoods near owned the market on those two commodities.

the natural

The family, which once had known only small-town Southern life, soon settled into its new urban home. Sonja would become a district manager for the H&R Block tax services chain; Willie, a music director for the Southland's Avalon Church of Christ. But their real jobs would come serving the dreams of their kids.

"They gave it all up so they could take me to auditions and [casting] calls, without knowing if I would be successful," Brandy remembered in *Seventeen*.

Sacrifice was part of the game. You didn't get something for nothing. You didn't get a shot at the top (of the pop charts, of the Nielsen ratings, of the box office—whatever) without risking sweat. Sonja and Willie knew that.

To the young, preschool Brandy, the concept of sacrifice was something that probably didn't figure yet. Performing was simply what came naturally . . . like breathing. No audience was too small, no gig too insignificant.

"She always had her play microphone," father Willie told *Vibe*. "Had her room set up for performances."

Brandy readily admits to having a thing for the spotlight.

"I'm a ham," she said in *USA Today*. "Once you get me going, I can't stop. I just love to perform. I love watching people's reaction."

In those early days her favorite forum—not counting that makeshift bedroom setup—was her father's church; gospel music, her first love.

Today, "One Voice," a standout cut from the *Never Say Never* collection, offers a glimpse of Brandy's affection for the genre. The rousing gospel-tinged number, featuring real-deal backup vocals by the likes of Christian artist BeBe Winans and Brandy's

Preceding spread and opposite: Brandy at the 1994 Lifebeat AIDS Benefit. (Copyright © 1994 Walter Weissman/Globe Photos, Inc.)

own music minister father, serves as a reminder of the little girl who grew up on the stuff of "Amazing Grace."

Had things turned out differently, maybe today Brandy would be gospel's hottest new act instead of a dominant force in the R&B and pop worlds. But things turned out differently.

One day, you see, the choir director's daughter saw a music video.

idol

It was 1986. Brandy was seven. She already knew she wanted to be a singer. She already was on her way, with an ever-growing number of choir performances under her belt.

Then she caught a video clip for a song called "How Will I Know?" It was an upbeat, poppy dance number by a new solo act. Name of Whitney Houston.

Brandy's life was forever changed.

"[In the video] she had on this tight skirt and this pink make-up on, and all this hair, and at that moment I knew I wanted to do that," Brandy recalled in *USA Today*.

Pink makeup may not seem the stuff of revelatory moments, but such things apparently catch the eyes of seven-year-olds. Brandy immediately recalibrated her ambitions.

Pretty soon, the chief thing she wanted to accomplish in her professional life, according to a 1996 on-line chat on the Black Entertainment Television Web site, was "to sell as many records as Whitney Houston."

In the mid-1980s, lots of little girls wanted to grow up to be Whitney Houston. (Arguably, there are probably a fair amount of people in the late 1990s who want the same thing.) But out of all those little girls, maybe Brandy was destined to have the best shot.

Like Brandy, Houston grew up on gospel music. She, too, learned firsthand the ins and outs of a song from a parent—in Houston's case, her mother, acclaimed singer (and former Elvis Presley backup vocalist) Cissy Houston.

Houston also moved easily through different worlds—singing, modeling, acting. In fact, like the future star of *Thea* and *Moesha*, Houston's very first taste of mainstream success would come in TV (with guest-starring stints on sitcoms like *Silver Spoons* and *Gimme a Break*), not the record stores.

To be sure, generational (Houston, born in 1963, is Brandy's

Whitney Houston, Brandy's greatest musical influence of all. (Copyright © 1998 Photofest)

elder by sixteen years) and geographic (Houston is an East Coast native) differences set them apart. But Brandy was not to be dissuaded.

"I'm very determined," she once told *Ebony*. "If I say this is what I'm going to do, I commit to that, and I do it."

Brandy wanted to be Whitney Houston. She was going to do it.

ups/downs

To be fair, Brandy didn't want to be *exactly* like Whitney Houston. After all, Houston was a grand old dame of twenty when her self-titled debut album was released in the summer of 1985.

Brandy wasn't keen on waiting until she hit double digits, much less turned twentysomething, before scoring her first hit record. She wanted it *yesterday*.

But—hate to bust your Cinderella bubble here—it didn't happen yesterday. It happened *slowly*.

With her ambition set and her parents' support in place, the young Miss Norwood embarked on a journey not recommended for the faint of heart or spirit. There were the local talent shows, the local charity events, the local church performances. And after those, some *more* local talent shows, local charity events, local church performances.

These gigs could be fun, but they couldn't be confused with glamour. They were all about down-and-dirty dues paying. They were all about honing skills. Building confidence. Even overcoming stage fright. (Yes, even confessed hams like Brandy know preshow jitters.)

Jeff Daniels battles a killer South American spider in Arachnophobia, *in which Brandy had a small role. (Copyright © 1990 Hollywood Pictures Company and Amblin Entertainment, Inc. Supplied by Photofest.)*

By 1990, Brandy was eleven and more determined than ever to join her idol Whitney Houston on the world stage.

She again went to her parents and told them she wanted into showbiz in a big way. Her parents responded in a big way, dedicating more time than ever to the matter of their budding in-house entertainers, including Brandy's brother Ray J, who by this time was also expressing desires to act and sing.

By year's end, Brandy was on her way. Even if it maybe didn't seem like that at the time.

First, she landed her first movie—a bit part in the Steven Spielberg–produced spider chiller *Arachnophobia,* starring Jeff Daniels and John Goodman. Whatever the role was intended to be on paper (notably, Brandy was cast to play a character *named* Brandy), on-screen it didn't amount to much. In the tradition of future A-list film stars like Kevin Costner (all but edited out of his "big break" movie, 1983's *The Big Chill*), Brandy's screen time was of the blink-and-you-missed-it length.

No matter, a movie *was* a movie; a real-live Hollywood job was a pretty cool thing. And though first a singer, Brandy looked at acting as another tool. Another way to get a foothold as an entertainer. Another way to get what she wanted.

Whatever it took.

"Acting at first didn't come naturally to me," she would later tell *Best of Rap and R&B* magazine. "[But] I love to be real and I love to be adventurous. I feel that in general, nothing ventured, nothing gained. You have to stick your neck out and do things."

Sometimes, Brandy wanted to blow up so big she just couldn't help herself. Mom Sonja remembers when her daughter was about eleven. The family attended a concert by bebopping rock legend Little Richard ("Tutti Frutti"). At one point, Richard asked the kids in the audience to join him onstage. Brandy took him up on his offer.

Big time.

The other children went one way on the stage; Brandy went the other. Off by herself, she took the opportunity to get in some practice . . . bowing. You know what? It felt pretty cool.

"She said, 'Mom, for a minute, I thought that was my audience,'" Sonja said in *USA Today.*

For one notable night in late 1990, they *were.* Brandy scored a dream opportunity for a starstruck little girl: being tapped to serenade a genuine star.

The star was comic actor Arsenio Hall, then host of his own groundbreaking late-night talk show.

The Brotherhood Crusade, a leading charity and activist group in Los Angeles, had named Hall its recipient of the Walter

Rock and Roll Hall of Famer Little Richard. (Copyright © 1998 Photofest)

Bremond Pioneer of Black Achievement Award. To perform in Hall's honor at his award dinner, the organization turned to Carson's own Brandy, dubbed "Darling" of the crusade.

For the big night, Brandy looked again to Whitney Houston for inspiration. She selected for her solo Houston's trademark power ballad, "Greatest Love of All."

The tune, about the power of believing in yourself, is something of a touchstone—maybe even good-luck charm—to Brandy and her industry peers. When she was thirteen, Monica—Brandy's "Boy Is Mine" duet partner—performed that very song at the showcase that helped *her* land a record deal.

Brandy's fortunes didn't rise so dramatically with her initial "Greatest Love of All" performance. Although it was warmly received by the audience, local coverage in the *Los Angeles Times* of the Hall dinner made no note of the young singer.

The early 1990s were a little like that for Brandy—she was working, she was doing, but was anybody *noticing*?

Yes and no. Local talent shows were starting to give way to TV appearances on programs like *Showtime at the Apollo*. Acting auditions were starting to translate into jobs in commercials.

It was all good, it just wasn't Whitney Houston-like.

Even if she wasn't in the hit-making business (yet), it was around this time that Brandy—still just eleven—laid down vocals on her first recordings. A producer who had spotted the aspiring singer at one of her assorted functions shopped the tracks to record labels. But nothing happened. By one account, record companies thought the still-developing Brandy sounded *too* much like her idol Whitney.

At this point it would have been easy for Brandy to give in to frustration—quit, pout, and otherwise get unproductive.

On one hand, yes, she was only eleven—hardly at the end of her rope. But on the other, she was powerless but to watch from the sidelines as other young performers—not much older, if not younger, than she—made big names for themselves.

The early 1990s were a good time to be a prepubescent R&B/hip-hop act—especially if you were a boy. In 1991, Prince protégé Tevin Campbell, all of fourteen, turned heads with the hit "Round and Round," from his debut album, *T.E.V.I.N.*

Kris Kross—the backward-dressing duo of "Jump" fame— were all of a combined twenty-four (that's twelve years apiece for members Chris Smith and Chris Kelley) when they jumped the charts in 1992.

Immature, an all-male R&B trio with roots dating back to the late 1980s, when the singers were still years away from teenhood, was another name player from this era, with hits like "Never Lie" to its credit. Without a solo career to call her own (yet), Brandy bided her time and briefly hooked up with the group as a backup singer.

In time (actually no more than a few years), acts like Tevin Campbell and Kris Kross and Immature would find the transition from kid-wonder acts to careers as enduring artists difficult, at best. (The record business, like certain other animals, has a nasty habit of eating its young.) But Brandy didn't have the benefit of

foresight. She didn't know what was *going* to happen. She could see only what *was* happening *now*.

Why them? Why not her? When was she going to get *her* shot?

Head-banging angst, though, has never been part of Brandy's MO. "When it comes to singing," she said on the *iMusic* Web site, "I've always been focused."

Maintaining that focus, Brandy and her mom, now her man-

ager, forged ahead. Brandy enrolled at the Hollywood High Performing Arts Center.

Finally, the Norwoods had arrived in Hollywood. But the realization of their dreams remained elusive. There was the teacher, for instance, who wouldn't even send Brandy on auditions.

"One day I asked, 'Why aren't you sending me out on calls?'" Brandy remembered in *People*.

"'Because you're not drop-dead gorgeous,'" the teacher answered.

"My heart just dropped."

Today, it's hard to imagine Brandy Norwood — whose braids, million-dollar smile, and impeccable duds make her a fashion idol from schoolyards to college campuses—could be discounted for alleged lack of style or looks.

But that's the way it goes sometimes—and, on that day at least, that's the way it went.

Certainly, Brandy, who has admitted to having a long memory, remembers the rejections. The slights.

"A lot of people used to tell me I wasn't going to be anything," she told the *Houston Chronicle* in 1996. "But all things are possible, if I believe and try hard enough."

Brandy believed. Brandy tried—hard.

Her reward was due.

Rap duo Kriss Kross in concert at Walt Disney's Epcot Center in Celebrate the Spirit! Disney's 4th of July Spectacular. (Copyright © 1992 The Walt Disney Company. Supplied by Photofest.)

chapter three **movin' on**

"I went from A–Z in this business. Now I know the ropes."

— Brandy

*I*n the Midwest, the year 1993 is remembered as the year of the Great Flood. It was an awful thing. The Mississippi River plain blew up—swelled, overflowed, busted loose. The mighty waterway and assorted tributaries left millions of acres of land sopping and useless.

Brandy plain blew up in 1993, too. But unlike the mess caused by the namesake river of her home state, this was *not* an awful thing.

In February, Brandy turned fourteen. She was starting to show the lithe, five-foot-seven-inch frame that would one day grace the pages of teenage fashion bibles.

She looked together—and she was *sounding* pretty together, too. The years of practice, auditions, more practice, and more auditions had honed her act. She was like the student who had enrolled in SAT

prep courses in the third grade. By high school, she was *ready* for the big test. She was ready to expand—in a positive way—just as the Mississippi River had that one year. . . .

big tests

In that magic year, there were two *key* auditions that lay ahead for Brandy. The first was for a regular role on a new network prime time series. The second, for a contract with a major record label.

Second things first: the record label audition.

In 1993, Darryl Williams was the A&R director for Atlantic Records. "A&R" is the music industry term for "artists and repertoire," and the A&R director is the suit who scouts, signs, and advises acts. As far as Brandy was concerned, Darryl Williams was the suit who "discovered" her.

Since Brandy had been knocking on doors for years, she was hardly an undiscovered country. Still, big time record contracts weren't exactly floating her way. It was Williams who finally summoned the newly minted teenager to an audition in Atlantic's Los Angeles offices.

She sang. Williams took note—of her energy, her poise, her voice.

"Brandy stood out," Williams would later tell *People*.

And so it happened. *Finally*.

Williams offered Brandy Norwood a record contract, offered her the chance to cut an album on the historic label home of soul great Aretha Franklin (who had recorded her classic "Respect" track with them), Hall of Fame rockers the Rolling Stones (during their *Exile on Main Street* days), and future home of new music acts like Jewel and Tori Amos.

And, maybe most importantly, Williams offered Brandy her best chance yet to make good on her Whitney Houston dream. She was going to be a professional recording artist—just like Whitney, who was riding as high as ever in 1993 with the record-setting chart topper "I Will Always Love You."

But first things first: back to that TV audition.

Brandy's agent set her up with a reading for a new show

called *Thea.* The would-be series was created by a man named Bernie Kukoff, who, fifteen years earlier, had launched Gary Coleman into stardom with *Diff'rent Strokes.* He later went on to serve as an executive producer of *The Cosby Show,* a favorite sitcom of the young Brandy. (Her TV-land goal was to be cute-as-a-button youngest daughter Rudy Huxtable.)

Like the prototypical sitcom of the pre-*Friends* 1990s, *Thea* was designed to be a vehicle for a stand-up comedian—think *Roseanne, Home Improvement* (Tim Allen), and *Grace Under Fire* (Brett Butler). In the case of *Thea,* the one-liner specialist was, appropriately enough, a comedienne named Thea Vidale.

In real life, Vidale was a mountainous, 235-pound force of nature with four kids. In her new sitcom life, Vidale was to be a mountainous, 235-pound force of nature with four kids.

Unlike the problem super-brats of *Married . . . with Children,* the children of *Thea* were drawn to be relatively attitude-free mortals who had their occasional rough spots ironed out by Mom. At the time, Brandy couldn't have written a show that would have played more to her strengths.

She read for the part of Danesha Turrell, the thirteen-year-old daughter of Thea (who, in the world of the sitcom, would be called Thea Turrell). The audition was in front of Vidale herself and the producers.

Brandy aced it. (Again.) The part was hers. The show got picked up.

She was going prime time.

Just like that, she had it. Or rather, she had *them:* a record deal, a TV show.

Brandy knew just what—and who—to credit for her remarkable two-for-two hot streak.

"I think it was the timing, the planning, the imaging," Brandy said, in the *Houston Chronicle.* "And God and my mom and dad."

first impressions

There *was* a downside to landing two great gigs at once: strange, but true. Brandy could do only one of them at a time.

Cutting a record is a full-time job. So is co-starring in a half-hour weekly TV series. While she would later swing that kind of double (even triple) duty during her *Moesha* run, the Brandy of 1993 wasn't the experienced Brandy of 1998. She was a talented, fourteen-year-old rookie finding her way in the big leagues. A little pacing would—and did—help.

Since TV had absolute time demands (the fall season, after all, must be served), the record deal went on the back burner. Brandy the singer would have to wait just a little longer. Brandy the actress was ready for her close-up.

"It was very, very hard," she later said of her inaugural sitcom experience, in an on-line chat on Black Entertainment Television's Web site. "But it taught me to be focused and to mind my own business."

Thea premiered on ABC-TV on September 8, 1993. (Eight days later, younger brother Ray J, billed as Willie Norwood, would make his own prime time series debut, on FOX's *The Sinbad Show*. The magic year, apparently, was spinning gold for the entire Norwood clan.)

The opening episode of *Thea* introduced viewers to the Turrell clan of Houston, Texas. Vidale starred as a widowed mom who worked two jobs—as a supermarket clerk and as a beautician—to keep food on the table and (somewhat) with-it clothes on the backs of her kids. Brandy (listed in the opening credits by her full name, Brandy Norwood) appeared as lone daughter Danesha. Acting-wise, her performance was a strong, slightly sassy, suffer-no-fools precursor to her future "It" girl days on *Moesha*. Fashion-wise . . . well, that was another story. Danesha Turrell was no precursor to Moesha Mitchell.

On *Thea*, Brandy was at the mercy of costumers who dumped her in panchos and jeans. (Granted, she *was* supposed to be the product of a financially strapped, single-parent home.) The look might have worked for character purposes, but it didn't exactly hint at the inner runway model. One thing, however, *did:* her hair.

Following a brief stint with a straight, flat bob that left her a dead ringer for Marla Gibbs's TV daughter on the NBC sitcom *227*, Brandy shifted to braids. They were shorter (chin length as opposed to down the back), but they were every bit the exotic

Rockin' the house at the New York Undercover *benefit. (Copyright © 1994 Walter Weissman/Globe Photos, Inc.)*

touch that would later set her apart from the multitude of skinny, blond girls gracing the covers of teen and fashion magazines.

"I never started out saying, 'I am Ms. Fashion Plate,'" Brandy would later tell *Best of Rap and R&B* magazine. "All I have done is have a fun time wearing what I wear and maybe venturing out onto a limb where other people don't."

Braids or no, on *Thea*, Brandy was just one of the bunch. She had three TV siblings with whom to compete for airtime. There was Adam Jeffries as eldest son Jarvis (the responsible one), Jason Weaver as middle son Jerome (the irresponsible one), and Brenden Jefferson as youngest child James (the cute one).

If there was to be a breakout star among the kid actors, judging by storyline focus, it figured to be the Gary Coleman-esque Jefferson or the flashy, scene-stealing Weaver. And although Weaver later ended up a Motown recording artist in his own right (as well as a co-star of the minor WB hit sitcom *The Smart Guy*), *Thea* was not to be a show where breakout stars were made. Even Brandy's vocals—she, along with Weaver, got to sing on a couple of early shows—didn't do much to raise the show's profile.

Episode titles like "Danesha's Project" and "Hair Today, Gone Tomorrow" pretty much tell the story: *Thea* was a *nice* show.

"Yields enough smiles . . . to warrant another look," wrote the *Los Angeles Times*'s Howard Rosenberg.

"Never objectionable, but also never exceptional," was the opinion of *USA Today*'s Matt Rousch.

That was about all they wrote. Brandy was virtually ignored in the notices, but she had company in neglect. To critics and audiences alike, *Thea* was a warm bowl of porridge—it wasn't too hot, it wasn't too cold, it wasn't the first thing you thought of when you got a craving for something tasty.

Good times to come: Brandy makes her grand entrance at the 1995 Essence Awards in New York City. (Copyright © 1995 Walter Weissman/Globe Photos, Inc.)

The show ambled along through a pretty forgettable TV year. The 1993-94 season was the stuff of such blink-and-you-missed-it programs as *Joe's Life*, *Second Half*, and *The Trouble with Larry*. (On second thought, if you blinked, you didn't really miss anything.)

But even a low-key show like *Thea* provided perks, like first—if not fire-breathing—fame. Not to mention steady paychecks.

"You know, when you get your first check, you think, 'Oh, my God, I'm rich!'" Brandy later related to *HX* magazine. "You scream and you want to go shopping! But you're not really rich, and you have to be careful."

Brandy had her mom to help her handle her money, but she was on her own where the future of *Thea* was concerned.

Only a handful of the some three dozen shows introduced that fall survived to the spring. *Frasier* and *Living Single* (the sitcom where Brandy's duet partner, Monica, would one day make her TV debut, albeit in a guest shot) were among the happy exceptions. *Thea* was not. The sitcom got cut down alongside the likes of Ray J's *Sinbad Show*, and a little-seen NBC family drama called *Against the Grain*, featuring future *Good Will Hunting* Oscar winner Ben Affleck.

The cited cause for *Thea*'s pink slip was the oldest story in TV: low ratings. Popular among the nation's 10.2 million black TV households (where it was the ninth most-watched series), *Thea* fared no better than fifty-third place overall. Pulled from the air in February 1994, it failed to make ABC's new fall lineup announced later that May. Its Wednesday-night time slot was filled by veteran actor Ed Asner's knee-slapper *Thunder Alley* (which also was axed not long after its debut).

Though not unexpected, *Thea*'s cancellation raised eyebrows among those who wondered if the show hadn't been short-changed because it featured an all-black cast. After all, *Boy Meets World*, another profoundly *nice* show (with an all-white cast), wasn't exactly a critical or Nielsen world-beater in its debut season, either, but *it* won renewal from ABC-TV.

To be fair, another kid-based sitcom on the network—*Phenom*, about a white, teenage tennis star—scored much stronger, much higher ratings than *Thea*, and it, too, failed to win a second sea-

Just a bat-fan at heart: At the premiere of Batman Forever. (Copyright © 1995 Fitzroy Barrett/Globe Photos, Inc.)

son. If there was a lesson to be learned from this blizzard of cancellations, it was that TV, like life, wasn't exactly fair.

And if there was to be a lasting legacy of *Thea* (other than marking the prime time debut of Brandy) it was that its demise, in part, prompted civil-rights leader the Reverend Jesse Jackson, in September 1994, to call out the networks for what he termed "institutional racism." He put the broadcasters on notice to develop and support shows that gave evidence of diversity. A year later, CBS-TV would give the go-ahead for the development of a sitcom pilot about the life and loves of a black teenager, name of Moesha. (Coincidence? Maybe, but sometimes even coincidences need a little inciting shove.)

But *Moesha* was down the road . . . and, in the end, a road that would lead to UPN, not CBS. The present, in early 1994, was about the ashes of *Thea.* Brandy the singer helped Brandy the actress cope with the loss—and even look at it as a plus.

"I was anxious to get back into the studio and pursue my dream," she told *USA Today.*

Brandy the thinker had the right idea.

On *Thea,* she was a supporting player. Sure, if the show had been a hit, she would have risen faster with it. (As it was, she garnered a Youth in Film nomination for her role.)

But when the series failed, Brandy was blown clear of the debris. *Thea* didn't go down in the books as *her* bomb. Rather, it was exactly the sort of thing that could be put in the log as a learning experience. Brandy learned what it meant to hold down a high-pressure job. She learned what it meant to reach for success in a business fraught with failure.

She *learned.*

"I wouldn't change a thing in my life," Brandy told *Best of Rap and R&B* magazine. "I went from A–Z in this business. Now I know the ropes."

With her commitment to *Thea* wrapped, Brandy was about to learn some new ropes: the music industry ropes.

She couldn't wait.

chapter four **happy**

"She's one of the baddest singers of the '90s."
—Boyz II Men's Wanya Morris

Okay, so Brandy was going to record an album. But what *kind* of album? Or, more precisely, what kind of *songs?*

It's the challenge—and curse—of the singer who doesn't have "slash-song-writer" attached to her title: you've got the voice, but you don't necessarily have the material. If you get good material, no problem—the voice can make it great.

But first things first: where to find the songs?

the goods

Brandy surrounded herself with a pretty good search team, led by Atlantic's Darryl Williams. The man who signed Brandy to the label took personal interest in his work-in-progress, signing on as the project's executive producer. Also key to the team were Kipper Jones and Keith Crouch, a pair of accomplished producers, songwriters, and music-makers. Jones had written cuts for the likes of Chaka Khan and Tevin Campbell, and produced songstress Vanessa Williams's 1991 album *The Comfort Zone.* Crouch produced records for Toni Braxton, gospel's CeCe Winans, and Boyz II Men. (He would later work with two other Brandy-related artists: brother Ray J and former *Thea* co-star Jason Weaver.)

Others would contribute tracks and talent (notably the production team known as Somethin' for the People for Nothin' Personal—veterans who helped launch the group II D Extreme a year earlier), but it was the quartet of Brandy, Williams, Jones, and Crouch who would click like no other.

Jones and Crouch, either as a duo or individually (with other songwriters), penned the collection's standout tracks:

• "Movin' On": The album opener. A cool, bouncy declaration of independence that grooves so 1970s it sounds positively *Rockford Files.*

• "Best Friend": A laid-back cut about forever-by-blood best friends. (This is the track Brandy would dedicate to Ray J.)

• "Brokenhearted": A controlled ballad about getting over the romantic dumps.

• "Baby": A straightforward paean to a girl's favorite baby (i.e., a cute boy).

• "I Wanna Be Down": The kind of song Janet Jackson might have recorded for *janet* or *The Velvet Rope.* This beat-heavy cut about a girl who longs to be in the cool crowd, and in with the cool boy, would have meshed well with Jackson's breathy, underplayed sound. (As it was, it did just fine by Miss Norwood.)

Never the slacker, fifteen-year-old Brandy chipped in on the songwriting front with the "I Dedicate" trio ("Parts I-III")—song

snippets that served as the album's recurrent theme. In it, Brandy remembered the people who, directly or indirectly, got her to that day and delivered her to that microphone: her dad, her mom, her brother, Aretha Franklin, and, yes, Whitney Houston. (The avowed Houston fan, in fact, never sounded more like her idol than with her powerful, gospel-tinged vocals on those tracks.)

And so it came to pass (thanks to no small amount of blood, sweat, and track sheets) that Team Brandy amassed a solid batch of tunes. It was stuff that from first to last reflected its artist. Even if, in the outside music world, the spring of 1994 was about Nirvana's Kurt Cobain (killing himself), Hole's Courtney Love (selling herself), and their extended family of grunged-out alternative rockers (depressing themselves), Brandy's music world was about *her* world: falling in love, falling out of love, fitting in, hanging with friends, hanging with family.

Was that world as "deep" as Cobain rhyming "married" and "buried"? Was it as "relevant" as Tupac Shakur rapping about prison? Never mind. It was what it was—and what it *wasn't*. Brandy *wasn't* a twentysomething white guy with a bad stomach and a drug problem. She *wasn't* a poetic and/or explosive gangsta with a "Thug Life" tattoo. What she *was* was a straight-A student who lived with her parents, shopped at Contempo Casuals, craved McDonald's french fries and cheeseburgers, and worshiped at the temple of Whitney Houston.

Early on, Brandy decided to sing about was what real *to* her and *about* her.

"I shouldn't have to apologize for being nice," she said in *Best of Rap and R&B* magazine. "Sometimes I feel bad about people thinking I'm a goody-goody, but you shouldn't have to slit your wrists . . . to be popular and sell records."

Doing it her way, Brandy put her voice where her heart was and started singing. Recording went down in Los Angeles area studios like Ameraycan in North Hollywood—a place where musicians the caliber of jazz-rock great Herbie Hancock ("Rockit") once grooved. Brandy was likely one of the younger artists to put down tracks there, but she didn't sound like it. She had a register, range, and rasp—a glorious rasp—that never betrayed her age. The resulting sound—a chilled-out cross between divas

Whitney and Janet—gave depth to material that might have sounded schoolgirl-shallow in lesser vibratos.

The best of her work was reflected in fourteen songs (including the three "I Dedicate" tracks), representing fifty-five minutes of solid, polished R&B.

Brandy Norwood had an album. It was to be called, simply, *Brandy*.

the image

In a music store, the album cover art tells you what the music (temporarily trapped inside the CD's jewel box) can't—namely, what the artist and record company are trying to sell. (As a rule, don't trust artists who insist they're not trying to *sell* anything. If they've released more than one album, they're selling.)

Point is, Brandy's first album cover was key. The stint on *Thea* aside, this was to be her first real face-to-face meeting with the public on a first-name, "Hi, I'm Brandy" basis. And know this: First impressions *count*. Madonna can make three more babies, move to a farm in Wisconsin, and take up wearing pinafores, but she's *still* going to be tagged as the bandanna-wearing "Boy-Toy"/"Material Girl" of her mid-1980s debut years.

So what was Brandy's image to be?

The songs on her CD indicated a youthful, hopeful innocence. Her sound indicated a mature R&B presence. Her birth certificate indicated a fifteen-year-old.

Okay, so how to package that? Do you sell her older? Younger? What?

And before you decide, know that a rival label has a fifteen-year-old singer in its stable, too. Her name is Aaliyah and she's got a star producer/performer at the control-room knobs in R. Kelly ("I Believe I Can Fly"). Her sound is Janet Jackson-y, too, except with a greater hip-hop twist.

Aaliyah's debut album, *Age Ain't Nothing but a Number*, hit stores in June 1994. Her image? From songs ("I'm Down," as opposed to Brandy's "I *Wanna* Be Down") to cover shot (all-black ensemble with shades—black, of course), the image is dead-eyed

and clear: age ain't nothing but a number, *fool*. I'm just as cool—probably even cooler—than you.

Nothing wrong with self-confidence, mind you. Hey, it worked for Aaliyah. She helped run the boys' club (Tevin Campbell, Immature, etc.) off the charts. She got next.

So, there you have it—that's the competition. If Aaliyah's moving records with an "I'm Down" attitude, is that the way to go with Brandy?

Well, no.

Brandy's *Brandy*, remember? You line her up against a wall, throw on shades and a beret, and you've got Brandy, at fifteen, posing as something she's not.

Now, you could go the other way—maybe try to attract a little attention with a Calvin Klein perfume-ad pose. Use some strategically buttoned clothing. (Hey, on *janet*, the aforementioned Miss Jackson's not wearing anything but her boyfriend's *hands*.)

But that's not going to work, because that's not Brandy, at fifteen, either.

"I don't want young girls to think you have to reveal yourself in order to sell records," Brandy told *Seventeen* in 1995.

In the end, in order to sell records, Brandy sold Brandy—the "Every Teen" in contrast to Aaliyah's "Never in Your Wildest Dreams."

Like Aaliyah's, Brandy's cover shot said it all, too. Except, in Brandy's case it said: I get an allowance. I shop at the mall. That's probably where I got this *Newsies* getup (Oliver Twist cap, suspenders, baggy pants, lace-up boots). In short, on *Brandy*, she didn't look unapproachable. She looked like the girl in homeroom—the nice one with the good skin and cool hair ("Where'd you get those braids!"). The image was a good match for the songs. It was a good match for Brandy.

It was *all* good.

As writer Dream Hampton would put it down in *Vibe* a couple years later on the subject of Brandy: "Have no doubt: Good girls finish first, stay longest, and make all the loot."

Aaliyah: Brandy's main recording competition for 1994. (Copyright © 1994 Zomba Recording Corp. Supplied by Photofest.)

the coming-out party

Brandy, the album, was released to stores on September 20, 1994. Brandy, the performer, was released into the stratosphere soon after.

Critically, the reviews (most referring to this first-a-singer/then-an-actress entertainer as an "actress-turned-singer" on the basis of her short-lived *Thea* gig) were strong:

> "The album is young, bubbly, and even sexy." —*CD Now*
> "[An] ultra-funky debut." —*USA Today*
> "Brandy has the pipes to become more than the latest teenage next-big-thing." —*People*

Even mixed reviews—like a two-out-of-four-stars judgment in the *Los Angeles Times*—couldn't ignore the obvious: Brandy was "a teenage newcomer with surprisingly mature chops."

But, hands down, the best notices Brandy got were from the public.

"I Wanna Be Down" was the first single off the album. According to music-biz magazine *Billboard,* it sold a "modest" 5,500 copies its first week out of the box. But it's amazing how fast good buzz can turn "modest" into "monster." By October 22, 1994, the song listed No. 1 on the R&B singles chart.

Almost as fast as lightning strikes.

A few months earlier Brandy could have been dismissed as a failed sitcom star. A wannabe singer. Now, she was Number One. A lifetime of dreams was not only coming true—it was *exceeding* expectations. Changes were in order.

Brandy's regular schooling was out; tutors (for a solid three hours a day) were in. Mom's full-time gig at H&R Block was out; her new full-time gig as "Momager" (mom/manager) was in. Brandy's idle hours at mallrat stores like Rampage and BCBG were (mostly) out; work and travel were in.

The reasons for the lifestyle overhauls were as evident as "I Wanna Be Down" climbing over songs from established vets like Anita Baker and Barry White. As evident as her first hit surpassing entries from peers Immature (the group with whom she'd done backup work) and Aaliyah (the singer with whom she'd been, by default, compared).

"I Wanna Be Down" had flat-out become the new anthem for young people on the eternal quest to *be* . . . cool/hip/accepted. The song even managed to topple a cut from Boyz II Men.

At the time, there were few acts hotter than Boyz II Men. The all-male quartet from Philadelphia had been a force since their 1991 debut album *Cooleyhighharmony. GQ*-stylish and classically talented, Mike McCary, Nate Morris, Wanya Morris (no relation), and Shawn Stockman once reigned on the singles' pop charts for three months—a record-setting thirteen weeks—with their inescapable ballad "End of the Road." Their record would be broken by Whitney Houston's equally inescapable "I Will Always Love You" remake, but that was okay. In 1994, they'd tie the *new* record (then fourteen weeks) with the single "I'll Make Love to You."

It was that very same untouchable hit that Brandy would touch up on the R&B charts in October.

Such events do not—and did not—go unnoticed.

Wanya Morris, then twenty, placed a phone call to this fifteen-year-old girl who was messing with BIIM's run of the road. The message: congratulations. Morris was among the first wave of celebrity well-wishers who saw something special—saw something of the future—in Brandy. Singers Karyn White ("The Way You Love Me") and Toni Braxton called, too. So did rap artist/actress Queen Latifah.

And Whitney Houston.

Apparently telling every interviewer with a pencil that Whitney Houston is your idol does the trick. Apparently gushing in the liner notes to your eye-catching debut album that Whitney Houston is the greatest singer in the world and you want to grow up to be just like her doesn't hurt, either.

Whatever the case, Whitney Houston called Brandy Norwood. Being a human and not a robot, Brandy—how should we say?—freaked.

To this day, she has said that just the *sound* of *the* Whitney Houston on the other end of a telephone receiver provokes the purest and surest of reactions: a scream.

"To have these people even know my name was such an honor," she said, in *Newsweek*. "I mean, I'm just little ole Brandy, and they're superstars."

Like it or not, quotes like that were fast cementing Brandy's appealing "good girl" image. Hey, this kid isn't just Every Teen. She's *Humble, Starstruck* Every Teen!

But Brandy fought to keep her head on straight. ("[Being famous] hasn't hit me yet," she said in an on-line chat on the BET Web site. "And I don't want it to ever hit me because I want to stay humble.") She was becoming something decidedly other than Every Teen.

"Little ole Brandy" was becoming a superstar, too—every bit as successful, if not more so, than her A-list mutual admiration society.

In November 1994, *Brandy* became a certified gold album—moving the required 500,000 units in just two months. It was well on its way to its eventual multi-platinum status . . . with *four million* copies sold.

This was getting a little unreal.

Brandy had started the year hidden in the cast of a floundering TV sitcom. She was ending it in the spotlight—on the charts and on the stage, where she performed a week of concerts in England with singer Keith Sweat ("I Want Her").

You want turnaround? This *was* turnaround: the no-name kid from Carson, California, getting booked on Johnny Carson's old haunt, NBC's *Tonight Show*. In December, she did the late-night thing with Jay Leno, singing "I Wanna Be Down" for a network audience.

The last day of 1994 was as good to Brandy as the last three months had been. On December 31, "I Wanna Be Down" climbed to No. 6 on the overall pop singles chart. She'd blown up as big on the mainstream music scene as Janet Jackson and Madonna, who also charted singles (*below* Brandy) that week.

On the R&B charts, she topped all comers—again—in February 1995. Her next single, the plaintive "Baby," soared to No. 1 even as "I Wanna Be Down" continued to hang on in the Top Ten. On the pop charts, "Baby" would fly even higher than its predecessor, landing at No. 4 one month later. It was Brandy's first Top Five hit.

"*The* soul sensation of the moment," *Newsweek* raved as it included Brandy in its early 1995 roundup of "New Faces for the New Year."

To hear her record company tell it, she also was the fashion sensation of the moment. Atlantic reported to *Seventeen* that it logged more than two hundred phone calls from girls who wanted to know what, how, and where they could get what were hereafter to be known as "Brandy braids."

Perhaps only someone like Jennifer Aniston of TV's *Friends* (she of the "Rachel cut") can appreciate that kind of influence. It's one thing to touch people with your work—it's another thing to make them want to *look* like you.

That is called going beyond the touching of a nerve. That is called reaching the outer extremes of *über*-celebrity power. And at that once-in-a-lifetime moment, you have two ways to go: (1) use your power for good; or (2) do whatever you want and pretend nobody cares.

Thing is, right or wrong, people *do* care about what their celebrities do. And nobody watches (or studies) more intently than kids. So, the pressure was on for Brandy. How was she going to handle it?

America need not have worried.

In late 1994, Brandy already was shouldering the role-model mantle on a tour of school campuses. She performed a little, she preached a little—stay in school, stay off drugs, do good.

All this was getting even *more* unreal, at least as far as some doubters were concerned. Was Brandy supposed to be perfect or something? Good voice? Best-selling record? Yeah, right. Probably washes her face with Ivory soap, too. (Well, actually . . . yes.) Had to be a put-on. *Had* to be. And that attitude—that "Brandy's a fraud" line—was probably one of the young performer's first brushes with the downside of fame.

"People don't expect to see somebody successful, young, and happy. That's just too much," she would tell *Mad Rhythms* magazine.

Welcome to *real* stardom—where image control goes only so far, and people think what they're going to think, say what they're going to say.

And it wasn't just Brandy. Even Aaliyah, who started out giving herself up as the anti-Brandy, got bad-mouthed, too. People saying she wasn't *really* fifteen. People saying she was secretly married to R. Kelly. Aaliyah denied both rumors—big time. But people talked. People *always* talk.

And people get jealous. And nosy. And think nothing of asking you about the intimate details of your private life. Who are you dating? Have you had sex yet? Brandy was dealing with this stuff at age fifteen. How many high-school sophomores jump at the opportunity to let the whole wide world in on their love life, or lack thereof?

Fortunately, Brandy wasn't like most high-school sophomores. With the help of her mom—always a shield against the media and showbiz types forever wanting a piece of her suddenly hot-property daughter—she managed to handle the scrutiny and absorb the pressure without going crazy. So for paparazzi and the press, she had only smiles.

The act—always being on, always minding your step, always having *somewhere* to go—could be tiring, even for a seasoned pro. Which Brandy wasn't. She'd been Brandy—*Star!*—for only a few months, tops. Sometimes, she admitted, she just wanted to stay home. Her mom would step in at those times, too.

"'Well, you wanted it,'" Sonja would remind her daughter, who repeated the words to the *Houston Chronicle*. And Brandy would suck it up and admit Mom was right. This *was* what she wanted.

"A regular fifteen-year-old girl doesn't get this kind of attention," she said in *USA Today* in 1995. "I can go to the mall anytime."

Not without causing a stir, she couldn't, because now she was BRANDY!

Capitals. Exclamation point.

Cover girl: Brandy holds up a copy of the April 1995 Seventeen *magazine. (Copyright © 1995 Lisa Rose/Globe Photos, Inc.)*

The winter of 1995 hardly chilled Brandy's bubbling career. "Baby" was cooking on the charts. *Soul Train* Music Award nominations were in the offing. *Seventeen* magazine was selling her as a cover girl. Queen Latifah, M.C. Lyte, and Yo-Yo were going into the studio to help Miss Norwood record a remix of her *first* hit, "I Wanna Be Down."

And then there was, perhaps, the topper: performing live shows on a bill with Boyz II Men.

Brandy was the opening act at these gigs—not the star—but this was not the time to quibble over billing. (Not that she wanted to.) This was a girl who started out in church choir, remember, and, suddenly—*bam!*—there she was, playing stadiums. The Spectrum in Philadelphia. The Omni in Atlanta. And she was doing it in the company of R&B royalty.

It was enough to make a teenager starry-eyed. (Or more so than usual.) And it did. Brandy developed a thing for BIIM's Wanya Morris. She liked the way he sang. She liked the way he listened. Wasn't too hard on the eyes, either. Wanya might have been known as "Squirt" to bandmates, but to Brandy, he was The First Big Crush.

Their age difference—Wanya had already gone from boy to man, while Brandy wasn't yet sixteen—kept things from getting any further than the "best friend" stage. Wanya treated Brandy like a kid sister. Good thing, too. According to *Vibe,* mom Sonja pledged to make BIIM a trio if Wanya acted anything *but* brotherly to her baby.

No drastic measures were needed. And like any good sibling, Wanya even pitched in for sis's birthday.

That February, Brandy spent her sweet sixteen weekend in Phoenix, Arizona. The occasion was work—but *what* work! Performing at All-Star Weekend for the National Basketball Association, mingling at celeb-packed events, singing the national anthem at game time. Not a bad gig.

Then it got better.

The night before the big game—almost a year to the day from when *Thea* had been dragged off to the Nielsen graveyard—

A "family" outing: Brandy and "older brother" Wanya Morris of Boyz II Men arrive at the New York premiere of Rodgers & Hammerstein's Cinderella. (Copyright © 1997 Andrea Renault/Globe Photos, Inc.)

Brandy got dragged into a party at the local Hard Rock Café. She didn't know it, but it was *her* party. Her record label was taking care of its own. (Particularly when its own sells four million records.) There was cake, diamonds, and "Happy Birthday," crooned by none other than Wanya and his Boyz II Men comrades.

"She's one of the baddest singers of the '90s," Wanya declared, according to a *Vibe* account of the night. "She's going to be out there for a long time."

A brother knows.

"The girl is me!"
— Brandy, on Moesha

Sacramento Kings hoops star
Mitch Richmond emerged from
the 1995 NBA All-Star Week-
end voted Most Valuable Player. Official-
ly, that is.

As far as killer performances went,
though, few could ace the one being pulled
off by Brandy that same year. Things were
staying sweet for the sweet sixteen girl.
Even minor scrapes—or scars, as the case
might be—didn't sting.

Take the fender bender at Los Angeles's Crenshaw High School. Brandy was
the campus's guest at a football halftime
show. As she explained to the *Los Angeles
Times*, she was heading out to the field via
a motor cart—the kind used to carry in-
jured players to the locker room—when

she literally ran into trouble. Brandy was driving the cart her very own self. Unfortunately, even superstars can have problems with steering.

"We went through a tunnel and I got too close to the wall," she told the newspaper. The result? A one-inch scar near an elbow. No biggie. Besides, she'd soon have *better* memories of Crenshaw High.

Brandy was due to return to the school . . . as student Moesha Mitchell.

about a girl

Prior to the 1990s, teenage girls—of all races, of all ethnicities, of all kinds—were the forgotten of prime time television. Conventional wisdom said girls didn't want to see other girls (whom they supposedly considered the much-loathed "competition"), even if they were the most interesting part of a show. Boys weren't supposed to want to see drippy ol' girls, either . . . unless, of course, they were falling out of bikinis.

Oh, sure, an occasional teenage girl would sneak into the spotlight. The 1960s had Sally Field's surf-loving *Gidget* and the squeaky-clean *Patty Duke Show*. The 1970s had . . . well, pretty much nobody. (Maureen McCormick and Susan Dey achieved demi-teen-idol status as eldest sisters Marcia on *The Brady Bunch* and Laurie on *The Partridge Family*, respectively, but both actresses were buried in multisibling sitcoms.) The 1980s had the *Facts of Life* girls, although, again, the focus was on the group, not the individual. About the closest that decade of boy-fronted shows like *Charles in Charge* and *Growing Pains* came to a prime time breakout star of the young, female persuasion was Lisa Bonet.

In 1987, *The Cosby Show* co-star—who played daughter Denise Huxtable—won her own spinoff series, *A Different World*, which placed her character in a college dorm. Here, ostensibly, was a choice opportunity to explore the rituals and traumas of freshman life through the eyes of an eighteen-year-old girl protagonist, years before stuff like *My So-Called Life* or *Felicity*.

But it was a choice opportunity blown. The comedy with

Bonet at center was tepid and lost. By the second season, she was gone, the focus shifting to seasoned ringers like Jasmine Guy. Guy, as preppy student-body standout Whitley Gilbert, was a skilled younger actress, but she was not a *young* actress. Teenage girls would have to wait for their champion.

Not to worry. She was coming.

"There was a void that needed to be filled," TV producer Sara V. Finney told the *Los Angeles Times.*

In 1995, Finney and partner Vida Spears were veterans of the prime time wars, with credits on shows such as *Family Matters* — yet another youth-oriented series where boys (even nerd bombs like Jaleel White's Steve Urkel character) got all the good lines and girls got all the roll-your-eyes reaction shots. Nothing personal against Urkel, but Finney and Spears wanted something different. They wanted to do a show about a teenage girl.

And with Ralph Farquhar they would. Farquhar was the creative force behind *South Central,* a well-reviewed but doomed 1994 Fox series that represented that equally rare prime time creature: the realistic, black-populated comedy/drama. The combination of Finney, Spears, and Farquhar would turn out to be a cool match. Before too long, CBS-TV, the home of beloved geriatric fare like *Murder, She Wrote* and *Diagnosis Murder,* had somewhat inexplicably commissioned a pilot from the trio.

Moesha was born.

Timing is to TV what location, cliché tells us, is to real estate: everything. The 1990s were as ripe for shows with female teen leads as the 1980s had been barren. Future *Sabrina, the Teenage*

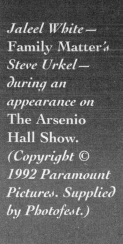

Jaleel White — Family Matter's Steve Urkel — during an appearance on The Arsenio Hall Show. *(Copyright © 1992 Paramount Pictures. Supplied by Photofest.)*

Witch star Melissa Joan Hart kicked in the door on cable as the sharp, appealing heroine of Nickelodeon's cult favorite *Clarissa Explains It All.* Mayim Bialik, who had a false start as leading lady material on Fox's failed teen sitcom *Molloy,* broke loose the hinges with *Blossom.* The NBC-TV sitcom, which debuted in January 1991, was unabashedly girlie. Bialik, all hats and flowers and funky clothes, literally pranced through the opening credits. But here was the kicker: on *Blossom,* it was Blossom who got the good lines.

My So-Called Life, starring Claire Danes, was another key player in this unofficial prime time version of Lilith Fair. That ABC-TV drama, about an angst-ridden fifteen-year-old girl with a bad dye job, failed to demonstrate widespread ratings appeal during its 1994–95 run. But that was a minor point. The *real* point was that the audience it *did* attract was loyal and—to most networks—demographically desirable (i.e., composed of teens with disposable allowances). In the end, it was no surprise when (a)

MTV swooped in to snatch up the reruns, and (b) Danes parlayed her teen martyrdom status into a film career (*Little Women*, *William Shakespeare's Romeo + Juliet*).

However, although hailing from different family backgrounds and possessing different temperaments, there *was* one trait that groundbreaking TV teens Clarissa, Blossom, and *My So-Called Life*'s Angela shared: they were all white.

Moesha Mitchell was going to be black.

The title character of CBS's in-development comedy project, Moesha was a fourteen-year-old Los Angeles-area girl coping with being a fourteen-year-old Los Angeles-area girl. She had a strict but loving dad (a car dealer for Saturn), a brand-new step-mom (her "real" mom was dead), a precocious, well-meaning baby brother, and a boy-crazy best girlfriend. That Moesha, her family, and immediate circle of friends (students at the aforementioned Crenshaw High) were black was not insignificant.

"When you're talking about a character, black is who Moesha is," producer Vida Spears said in *Word Up!* "The show would be different had Moesha been white."

But the fact that Moesha was black was not to be the be-all, end-all of the series, either. Her stories, narrated in her own voice, ideally would appeal to all audiences—black, white, whatever. If things went by plan, Moesha Mitchell was going to be TV's first Every Teen of color.

But who was going to be Moesha?

CBS wanted a star—that's usual network thinking. But *Moesha* was not your usual project. It's 1995: go name five stars black, female, and approximately fifteen years old. The list pretty much started and ended with Brandy Norwood. Her agent fielded the requisite call.

"At first I said, 'What kind of name is Moesha?'" Brandy recalled in *Newsweek*. "After I read the script I was like, 'The girl is me!'"

The *Moesha* camp caught a break. Brandy clicked with the project—even if "a project" was the last thing the newly acclaimed recording artist was seeking.

"I was a singer and I didn't want to act," she said in *Jet*.

Choices, choices.

matter of principle

In July 1995, Brandy scored yet another hit off her debut album. "Best Friend," the Ray J tribute, rose to No. 7 on the R&B singles chart. That October would bring still more success: "Brokenhearted" moved to No. 2 in the R&B division and an impressive ninth place on the overall pop singles chart.

Brandy had become nothing less than a gold mine. Funny thing, though, about a winning streak in the notoriously fickle music business—the question that people ask isn't "How long can it continue?" but "When will it end—and how miserable an ending will it be?"

The fates (and fans) are particularly unkind to artists who depend on the kindness of young listeners. (Know anyone who still avidly collects Joey Lawrence music?) While there's no small accomplishment in scoring one hit record or one hit album, it still hurts when people who lavished praise on you one year can so completely ignore you the next. In music, a popularly prescribed course of preventive medicine is to strike early and often.

Ever wonder why the bubblegum popsters of the Spice Girls released two albums and a movie in the first eleven months of their U.S. invasion? Or why the "MMMBop" boys of Hanson blitzed the market with *three* albums—including an "early years" retrospective—a mere twelve months into their debut? They were striking early . . . and often.

The smart money said Brandy would—should—do the same. Hurry—find some new songs. Quick—cut that second album. Fast—before the public finds a new "Baby."

The smart money was wrong. Brandy was in this game—showbiz—for the long haul. There was to be no rushing, no forced moves.

"I like doing it all—singing, television, movies," Brandy told *Jet*. "Everything that's hard I want to do."

Putting her long-awaited record career aside for a television series was, indeed, going to be hard. But, as before, Brandy the singer deferred to Brandy the actress. She liked the script. She signed up. Her prime time opportunity was a go.

Brandy takes the stage at the 39th Annual Grammy Awards, held in New York City. (Copyright © 1997 John Barrett/Globe Photos, Inc.)

Well, *almost* a go. The *Moesha* pilot got filmed. Got delivered to the network.

Got rejected.

CBS told the producers that the comedy didn't mesh with its audience—that being old, older, and support-hose-wearing oldest.

"They wanted to do a whole other show without the cast," Brandy told the *Mr. Showbiz* Web site. "I didn't want to do that."

Brandy and company stuck to their principles. They bet that there *was* an audience for a series about a young, strong, teenage girl who just happened to be black—and who happened to be proud of it.

Cue the United Paramount Network.

To understand *Moesha*'s place in the TV universe is to understand its roots . . . and those of UPN.

UPN was—still is, really—a mini-network, launched on January 16, 1995, with a mere two nights' worth of weekly programming. (It expanded that reach to five nights a week, effective the 1998-99 season.) The venture was backed by Hollywood's Paramount Pictures—the *Star Trek* people. The network's first regular show was to be (what else?) another *Star Trek* show—this one subtitled *Voyager.* The UPN's chief rival was—still is—the WB, the *other* mini-network also born in January 1995. The WB was backed by Warner Bros.—the *Batman* people.

Using the blueprint drafted by FOX-TV a decade earlier, UPN and the WB sought to lure viewers away from the Big Three networks (ABC, CBS, and NBC) by scheduling stuff that the Big Three didn't. In the beginning, that meant sophomoric sex comedies for the WB (*Muscle*) and male-oriented action shows for UPN (*Marker*).

Soon the two upstarts would rush to serve another underserved market: the black audience.

There was a time (read: the 1970s) when the Big Three were better about developing black comedies. Comics Bill Cosby, Redd Foxx, and even the four-letter-word-prone Richard Pryor all got their shots at prime time series for ABC, CBS, or NBC.

By the mid-1990s, Cosby, whose Jell-O commercials, if nothing else, were testament to his broad, cross-cultural appeal, was

the only player still considered employable by the Big Three. Okay, Foxx was dead, but Pryor? Even if ill health hadn't forced him into unofficial retirement, there didn't seem a chance that his once-edgy humor would be given prime time play in the brave new network world.

Fact was, the era of the integrated sitcom—even the integrated network—was ending. The new look could be seen, for example, in NBC's top-rated (in white homes) Thursday-night lineup: *Seinfeld, Friends, Frasier,* etc. The new look could be seen in FOX's top-rated (in black homes) series: *Martin, Living Single, Roc*, and others.

Into this divide came UPN and the WB. Lacking successful early identities (just about all their new shows, with the exception of *Star Trek: Voyager*, failed to do anything in the Nielsen ratings), they cribbed even more heavily from a portion of FOX's game plan and backed numerous black sitcoms. *Malcolm and Eddie, The Jamie Foxx Show, The Parent 'Hood* (an early 1995 entry), *The Wayans Brothers* (another 1995 vet), *Sparks, Good News, Sister, Sister* (canceled by ABC and revived by the WB), and the infamous *Homeboys in Outer Space* all popped up on the mini-networks.

So did *Moesha*.

After CBS passed on the pilot, UPN got into the groove. It wanted the show—the way it was. With Brandy. With everybody—a cast that included TV, film, and stage veteran William Allen Young as Moesha's dad, Frank Mitchell; original Broadway *Dreamgirls* diva Sheryl Lee Ralph as the stepmom, Dee Mitchell; young Marcus T. Paulk as her brother, Myles Mitchell; life-force teen actress Countess Vaughn (*Hangin' with Mr. Cooper, Roc*) as the boy-crazy bud, Kim Parker; Lamont Bentley as the Mitchells' forever-famished next-door neighbor, Hakeem Campbell; and Yvette Wilson (a *Thea* alum) as Andell, the owner of the local hangout, The Den. Soon to be added as full-timers were Shar Jackson as gal-pal Niecy, and Fredro Starr as Moesha's moody, sometimes/sometimes-not boyfriend Q. The belief seemed strong that with the right team in place, the audience and all that meant (press, ratings, influence, etc.) would follow, no matter *what* channel on the dial broadcast the show.

Faith was served.

Within a month of its debut, *Moesha* was winning its time slot against all comers—Big Three network shows included—in major cities like Miami, and drawing strong numbers in places like Los Angeles. No less than *Newsweek* declared it a "surprise hit" and an authentic one at that, praising producers for "keeping it real" and telling the life of a black teenage girl without getting either too storybook or too down.

Moesha was "real," all right—the "real" deal. The most popular new show on UPN, save for the road-tested *Star Trek* franchise. It proved that nonbelievers who had doubted the appeal of the series' hip-hop sensibility (which celebrated black culture, but not to the exclusion of nonblack culture) were wrong.

"It's the kind of show that people have been wanting for many years," co-star Willam Allen Young said in the *New Pittsburgh Courier*. "And not just African-Americans, but families of all colors."

star!

The exact premiere date of *Moesha* was January 23, 1996—otherwise known as the outset of the Year of Brandy.

Well, all right, you couldn't find that notation on calendars, but that doesn't make it any less true. Look, 1994 was pretty good, 1995 was even better, but 1996—only three weeks in—was looking *exceptional*. To dispense with the obvious, Brandy had a new TV show—*her own* TV show—and a best-selling (still) album.

The new year brought new perks—like a Grammy nomination. Even as she was ready to go global as a prime time star, Brandy was up for Best New Artist at February's Grammy ceremony. The category elevated her to a Heavyweight Class contender against rockers Hootie & the Blowfish ("Hold My Hand"), reformed teeny-bopper/presently moped-out singer Alanis Morissette ("You Oughta Know"), folkie Joan Osborne ("One of Us"), and country star Shania Twain ("There Goes the Neighborhood").

As it turned out, Morissette took the honor. But, as it also turned out, Brandy was a winner anyway. Six nights after *Moesha* debuted, on January 29, 1996, Brandy was named Favorite New Soul/R&B Artist at the American Music Awards.

But wait, there was more. There was a batch of *Soul Train* Lady of Soul awards (honoring—like the name says—female R&B, soul, jazz, and rap acts): four in 1995, including R&B/Soul Album of the Year; and one in 1996—the prestigious Entertainer of the Year, presented by the Reverend Jesse Jackson.

And then there was Whitney Houston. And Babyface.

In 1995, producer/writer/performer Kenneth "Babyface" Ed-

monds, an unstoppable Grammy-winning machine, was enlisted to help craft a soundtrack for Houston's upcoming film, a chick flick supreme called *Waiting to Exhale*. Edmonds, in turn, recruited an all-star stable of R&B artists to contribute tracks. Mary J. Blige, Toni Braxton, Aretha Franklin, Chaka Khan, Patti La-Belle, and TLC were on board. So was Houston, of course.

And so was Brandy.

"I'd never met Brandy other than in passing," Babyface told

Ebony. "But I knew what kind of artist she was. I knew how she sounded."

To Babyface, she sounded right for "Sittin' Up in My Room." A catchy track about a girl literally sittin' up in her room until the love of her life gets around to giving her a phone call, it *was* a perfect match for "Brokenhearted" Brandy. She made the thing sing.

And by the time her stint in the studio was done, it was Whitney Houston thanking *her* in the liner notes.

The soundtrack—hailed as one of the year's best albums by *The New York Times* and *Spin*—hit stores in November 1995. Houston, being co-executive producer, had the honor of the first single, "Exhale (Shoop Shoop)." By the turn of 1996, Brandy had her turn: "Sittin' Up in My Room" got the single treatment. By March, it had climbed to No. 2 on the pop chart.

Yeah, 1996 was working out okay.

And was the part about Brandy being adopted by *People* magazine mentioned yet? No? Well, the adoption wasn't official or anything—it just seemed like the editors there took Miss Norwood under their wing. They sure doted on her enough.

During a one-year run of the weekly magazine, *People* included Brandy in its roundup of best-dressed celebrities ("You can tell she adores being in front of the camera," ex-*Today* anchor Deborah Norville mused for the magazine), its roundup of the "Most Fascinating People on TV," and its roundup of the "Most Beautiful People." In the waning days of the millennium, that last honor was akin to being formally anointed by the celebrity gods. If—and when—you made the "Most Beautiful" cut, you were most golden.

Brandy was most golden.

Already a teen idol for her record success, the intimacy afforded by a weekly television series allowed Brandy to forge an even deeper bond with fans.

"I'm proud that little girls look up to me," she said in *Jet*. "Not to be boastful, but I think I'm a pretty good person to look up to." As she explained to the magazine, Brandy, like her TV self, was "very responsible," "positive," and a conscientious student.

In short, just like in her music, Brandy was not faking it on *Moesha.*

Brandy with TV parents Sheryl Lee Ralph and William Allen Young in the Moesha *episode "Road Trip." (Copyright © 1996 UPN. Supplied by Photofest.)*

This is not to say Brandy *was* Moesha. (Hard to imagine Brandy being shipped off to a private school because she was caught in an ill-advised, if innocent, scene with a boy in her room, as happened to the oft-defiant Miss Mitchell in the second and third seasons.) But, at a certain level, Brandy undeniably connected with Moesha.

"She brings complete legitimacy to the part of a teenager," Ralph Farquhar told *People.*

"Legitimacy" was the mantra of *Moesha* from the start. Co-star Countess Vaughn said the writing staff helped keep all the actors on the level—and, in turn, the actors helped keep the scribes on the level.

"We have older writers and we have younger writers, too, but sometimes the older ones go off a little bit and we go, 'Ummmm, we don't say that anymore,'" Vaughn told the *Jacksonville Free Press*.

Accordingly, there were few false beats during those early *Moesha* episodes. (Okay, maybe The Den seemed a little *too* perfect a hangout. Or maybe Mr. and Mrs. Mitchell seemed a little *too* nonstop lovey-dovey.) But a show that regularly attracted musical guests the likes of Black Street, Xscape, A Tribe Called Quest, and M. C. Lyte was doing its best to keep it legitimate. (And yet to come: Usher.) About the only hot R&B act that *didn't* pay a visit to Moesha's corner of Leimert Park in Los Angeles was Brandy.

Staying true to character at the expense of hyping would-be hit singles, Brandy didn't go around trying to squeeze in places for Moesha to show off her voice . . . like so many singing doctors on *General Hospital*. It was *Brandy* who had the voice, not Moesha Mitchell, and that's the way it was played. Brandy was the superstar who sang the *Moesha* theme song; Moesha was the civilian teenager who listened in awe to the guest acts.

Brandy seemed to like the division—being plain old Moesha let her be the young adult her career often wouldn't. As she told *Newsweek*, "On one show, I tried out to be a cheerleader, and it hit me that this was about the only way I'd ever get a chance to."

the prom

There was other stuff that Moesha got to try that Brandy didn't— like, date.

At age seventeen, Brandy's crush on Wanya Morris was still that—a crush. It was no more a real romance than her other stated crushes on the likes of rap mogul Sean "Puffy" Combs, a.k.a. Puff Daddy. She spoke of being sheltered, both by her family and by her lifestyle. She was a young person on the go, with lots of things to do, lots of places to go, and not lots of kickback time. It figured that when a teenager like Brandy finally got busy on the dating scene, she wasn't going to be bound by the usual dinner-and-a-movie route.

Prom Night: Brandy and date Kobe Bryant arrive at Bryant High School's prom, held at the Bellevue Hotel in Philadelphia, PA. (Copyright © 1996 Bruce Cotler/Globe Photos, Inc.)

She wasn't.

Her rookie suitor, for instance, stood six feet, seven inches tall.

Kobe Bryant was a nationally recognized high-school basketball star from Pennsylvania who made headlines in early 1996 by announcing his intention to skip college and offer his shooting services directly to the NBA. He was all of seventeen.

Before heading off to the arms (and elbows) of Charles Barkley and company, Kobe decided he, like Brandy, wanted to do some everyday, regular ol' teenager stuff. Kobe decided he wanted to go to his senior prom.

And he wanted to go with Brandy.

To the no-heart outsider, a superstar coupling—from Bruce and Demi to Brandy and Kobe—looks suspicious. Is it love, like, or a career move? Do they think they're too good to date "normal" people? What's their problem?

Perhaps their problem, in the case of Brandy and Kobe, was that they were seventeen and being watched by no-heart people with heavy-duty suspicions. Together, at least, they could talk about that stuff. Kobe looked to Brandy for advice. He was a newcomer on the national stage. She knew how to navigate the shoals of celebrity. The way Kobe saw it, Brandy—and maybe only Brandy—understood where he was at.

"A lot of things I'm going through, she's already been through," he later told *TV Guide*.

It was true: Brandy and Kobe were prodigies from the same overachieving mold. Where she had been belting out gospel songs at preschool age, he was shooting baskets and pretending to dunk at age three. Where she was inspired to pursue music by her choir-directing dad, he was inspired to follow in the path of his NBA veteran dad, Joe "Jellybean" Bryant. Where she was unshakable in the belief that she was to become a world-class entertainer, he was equally convinced that basketball was in his blood.

Then there were special Kobe bonuses, like how he spoke fluent Italian, which came from spending his formative years in Europe, where his father had extended his own career in the pro leagues. Or how he respected women, the by-product of growing up in a house with a mom and two older sisters. (Once he made his big pro money and bought his big, fancy pad along the California coastline, he even asked his family to move in with him.) There were a lot of reasons for Brandy to accept Kobe's May 1996 invite. And she did.

The senior prom of Lower Merion High School in Ardmore, Pennsylvania, awaited.

Brandy's parents allowed the would-be NBA star to whisk their daughter off on a three-day East Coast excursion—including a stay at an Atlantic City hotel—for this mega-sized prom date. The trust was well-placed: Brandy and Kobe's date, from first to last, was all very proper and extremely G-rated, down to very separate hotel rooms.

Brandy said Kobe was the model escort. "He picked me up, opened doors, brought me flowers, took me to a concert [by romance-meister Barry White], brought me to my hotel room at a decent hour," she told *Mad Rhythms* magazine. Complete with a hug and a chaste kiss to the cheek, it was, she said, "the perfect date."

The prom went just as smoothly . . . or as smoothly as could be expected. If Kobe was hoping to show up at the event and casually introduce his date ("Oh, by the way, this is Brandy, the best-selling singer and talented star of TV's *Moesha*"), he had arrived at a rare miscalculation.

The envy that certain classmates unleashed on Brandy back when she first started to make it big time staged a comeback at Lower Merion. Some students sounded off to reporters, vowing, as reported in the *Las Vegas Sun*, to "get up and leave" when Brandy and Kobe arrived. It was argued that the super-couple's presence would be "very disruptive." Brandy additionally took heat from those who charged she was using the prom as a publicity stunt. (Never mind that *Moesha* pretty much took care of her publicity needs those days.)

In spite of the media glare, in spite of the snipers, Brandy and Kobe had a good time. And then the prom was over, their "date" was over, and the two went their separate ways.

Brandy had *Moesha*, not to mention college. (Yeah, college. She wasn't amassing those straight-As for nothing.) After years

of private tutors, Brandy returned to a campus setting in the fall of 1996, enrolling in Pepperdine University, a private Christian institution located in Malibu, California. Her major: psychology.

Kobe, meanwhile, had the NBA, where he was drafted later that summer by the expansion-league Charlotte Hornets and then quickly traded to the storied Los Angeles Lakers. Kobe signed a three-year, $3.5 million deal with the glamour team. Previously a novelty of the sports pages, Kobe was now on his way to becoming a full-fledged media star. He had a sneaker deal and an agent and everything.

But he didn't have Brandy.

He filmed a guest shot on *Moesha* for the fall of 1996, but that was about it as far as quality time with his ex-prom date went. For whatever reason—and in interviews, Brandy was unable to pinpoint a cause for their separation—the two fell apart. On the romantic front, anyway.

They *did* remain friends, however. And they *did* remain in touch. Being partners in high-profile happenings, it was pretty hard to lose sight of each other's accomplishments. Brandy, in particular, delighted at seeing Kobe excel in the pros. (He was no less than a starter by the 1998 All-Star Game.)

In some ways, she felt Mr. Bryant, during their but one date, spoiled her for future leading men. The guy was just plain a gentleman.

As she told *Black Beat*, "I would marry a guy like Kobe Bryant."

Brandy holds hands with Kobe Bryant at the premiere of the Arnold Schwarzenegger/ Vanessa L. Williams action movie Eraser. *(Copyright © 1996 Lisa Rose/Globe Photos, Inc.)*

back to work

It was time for Cinderella to put away the prom dress and get back to Moesha's locker. A second TV season beckoned.

The demands for a second solo album beckoned, too, but Brandy temporarily ignored those calls. As early as the spring of 1996, the press speculated about her heading back to the studio to record her sophomore collection. Surely, she wasn't going to chuck music entirely for TV.

No, surely, she wasn't. But Brandy would later admit that she was hesitant about cutting the second album. The fear—the doubt—was palpable: what if she didn't have the elusive *it* anymore?

Of course, one of the reasons it's good to be Brandy is that Brandy's always got something cooking. Don't feel like you're up to recording new songs? Why not retreat to the newfound security of your prime time TV family? Brandy did just that—immersing herself in the show, working on character, improving her acting, learning to carry scenes with more ease. On *Moesha*, at least, Brandy didn't have to worry about the sophomore slump. The show was stronger than ever, dispensing little life lessons amid its sassy punch lines. In a TV year where many black sitcoms were being trashed for falling to the depths of buffoonery, dignified *Moesha* kept its head high, kept its mission in sight: this comedy was *real*. Helping keep Moesha Mitchell real was a now regular love interest—a cueball-domed guy name of Q—which helped the show explore dating issues.

Again, Brandy was living vicariously through Moesha. The Kobe prom aside (and, really, that was a onetime, friendly date thing), Brandy hadn't hooked up in the romance department with a steady guy. Crushes aside, she hadn't fallen truly, deeply in love.

All that would change, however, in February 1997, on the occasion of Brandy's eighteenth birthday.

Finally, Brandy—not Moesha—was going to get the guy.

chapter six **fairy tales**

"My mom had to pinch me."
— Brandy

In 1997, Brandy knew how to throw a bash for her eighteenth birthday. The scene: The House of Blues on Los Angeles' famed Sunset "Strip." The guest list: friends (including Pepperdine classmates), family, cast members of *Moesha*, NBA standout Penny Hardaway, *Family Matters* star Jaleel White (yes, the Urkel guy), former prom date Kobe Bryant, and former crush Wanya Morris.

That night, however, one of Brandy's "former" guys wasn't sounding so "former."

"It's a party honoring a beautiful person," Wanya told *People* magazine. He'd been invited to Brandy's adult coming-out party by Brandy herself. She telephoned. He accepted.

Something clicked.

boyfriend

When Wanya first met Brandy, remember, she was a kid. A pretty cool kid, yeah, but a kid all the same. To make matters worse, Brandy had once experienced a typically awkward (and somewhat embarrassing) adolescent moment in the presence of Wanya and his Boyz II Men compatriots. It was at one of the gigs when she was working the same bill with the quartet. There was some water on the stage—a remnant of the Boyz' "Waters Run Dry" number. Brandy's foot met water and—*bam!*—Brandy's body met stage.

"I slipped and fell and did, like, a total split," she told *Teen People.* "It hurt really bad."

But that was then; *this* was 1997. Brandy wasn't a cute, up-and-coming performer anymore. She was an up-and-staying star. And her girl-next-door cuteness was morphing into a woman-next-door litheness.

Wanya noticed. Little sister had grown up—and he didn't think of her as a "little sister" anymore.

Brandy, who'd done her share of dating as her TV self on *Moesha,* now had her first real-life boyfriend. She was eighteen. He was twenty-three. Together, they made for a paparazzi-perfect young power couple—a magnet for the flashbulb. They attended premieres. They made *Ebony's* "10 Hottest Couples" issue, right alongside old married folks Will Smith and Jada Pinkett.

Brandy didn't talk a lot publicly about the details of the relationship. (A little privacy, please.) But by all appearances, through 1997, the twosome appeared solid and together . . . as much as their careers would allow.

Where Brandy was concerned, however, the career didn't allow much time in her life for more than the ever-expanding career itself.

friend

Summer 1997 brought another back-to-work schedule for *Moesha,* then entering its third season. The show was moving its focus

Preceding spread: The cast of Rodgers & Hammerstein's Cinderella: *(left to right)* Jason Alexander, Paolo Montalban, Brandy, Whitney Houston, Bernadette Peters, Natalie Desselle. (Copyright © 1997 ABC-TV. Supplied by Photofest.)

Opposite: Brandy with Wanya Morris at the 10th Annual Soul Train Music Awards. (Copyright © 1996 Fitzroy Barrett/Globe Photos, Inc.)

to the largely white private school where Moesha was enrolled—against her wishes—after a major run-in with her father over her boyfriend, Q. As Brandy's fortunes in the love department had changed for the better, so would Moesha's. Out of the picture on the TV boyfriend front (sort of) was Q; in the picture, as the character's new sometime love interest, was Usher.

Usher needed no introduction to *Moesha*'s plugged-in younger viewers. He was part of her elite celebrity peer group—a one-named, teenage, best-selling R&B star.

Born in 1978, Usher Raymond (yes, that's the way it appears on his birth certificate) was an overachiever in the Brandy mold. Signed a record deal when he was fourteen. Camped out with Puff Daddy during production. Smiled his dimpled grin all the way up to pinup-poster stardom.

Usher didn't bust as big out of the box as Brandy did. His self-titled debut album, released in 1994, did all right, yielding the gold single "Can U Get Wit It," and drawing mostly positive critical feedback. But it wasn't the clear-cut breakthrough that *Brandy* had been. That would come in time—with the 1997 launch of his second album, *My Way*, to be precise. Fueled by the Grammy-nominated hit "You Make Me Wanna . . .", Usher was on his way—going triple platinum, touring with Janet Jackson, and making his washboard stomach and bare chest even more famous than his trademark grin. As with Brandy, big-time success brought modeling offers (for Tommy Hilfiger), magazine covers, and acting opportunities—one of which included *Moesha*.

On *Moesha*, Usher was cast as Jeremy, the clean-cut (no abs-flashing required here), varsity-approved alternative to malcontent Q. It wasn't a regular gig, but it was good enough to get people talking: what was up with Brandy . . . and Usher?

The answer: nothing.

"We're just very good friends," Usher said in *Black Beat's Ultimate Usher*. The oldest line in show business, right? Maybe, but give the guy a break. Sometimes a denial really *is* a denial — and *not* an evasion.

The way Brandy tells it, she doesn't even like to tell Usher she likes his music (which she does), so—you know—he won't go thinking she likes his music. If that sounds more like a sister-brother teasing thing than a starry-eyed romantic thing, then good. Because that's the way it is. And was. By all accounts, Brandy and Usher were no more than co-workers on the *Moesha* set—admiring co-workers.

"She's fine, and there's no one nicer, smarter or more together in the business," Usher told *Black Beat's Ultimate Usher.* "She's got it going on."

In a strictly professional sense, of course.

crowned

Brandy never met composers Richard Rodgers and Oscar Hammerstein II, but they became pretty important guys in her life, too.

Rodgers and Hammerstein were, in their hit-making days—chiefly, the 1940s and 1950s—*the bomb*. (Not that anyone would have called them that back then.) If you've seen *The Sound of Music* (the movie with the nuns, the Nazis, and Julie Andrews), you know their stuff. Same goes with *Oklahoma!* And *Carousel*. The songwriting duo (Rodgers wrote the music; Hammerstein hammered out the lyrics) crafted a whole wing of modern American song standards unto themselves through their Broadway (and, later, filmed) creations. "Oh, What a Beautiful Morning." "Edelweiss." "Climb Every Mountain." *That's* Rodgers and Hammerstein.

In the late 1950s, the guys knocked off a score for that upstart

Smiling that dimpled grin: Usher at the 12th Annual Soul Train Music Awards. (Copyright © 1998 Fitzroy Barrett/Globe Photos, Inc.)

medium, television. The project was *Cinderella*, the age-old fairy tale about an overlooked girl who overcomes a lousy stepmother, lousy stepsisters, and a dusty wardrobe to bag the No. 1 bachelor in all the land (with the help of a fairy godmother and a pumpkin carriage).

Julie Andrews (the *Sound of Music* movie lady, remember?) got first crack at the material—including soaring songs like "Impossible." She starred in the inaugural television production, which was broadcast on March 31, 1957, on CBS. There was something in the combination of its pedigree, its star, and its story that made for instant event viewing. *Rodgers & Hammerstein's Cinderella* was a hit.

The musical made its second TV appearance on February 22, 1965, with then-newcomer Lesley Ann Warren doing the gown-and-glass-slipper routine in a restaged and in-living-color remake for CBS. Another TV classic was christened.

For more than thirty years, Warren was the tube's reigning Cinderella. (Unless you count 1978's *Cindy*, an all-black Cinderella tale set in Harlem. But that ABC production wasn't based on the Rodgers and Hammerstein version.)

Even as Warren went on to other parts (an Oscar nomination for 1982's *Victor, Victoria*, for example), she was forever linked in the minds of TV-addled baby boomers with that night back in 1965 when she waltzed with Prince Charming (future *General Hospital* soap star Stuart Damon).

America, clearly, had a thing for its Cinderellas.

Fast forward to the late 1990s. Whitney Houston, feeling entrepreneurial between her film and recording work, was working with the Disney people on an all-new *Cinderella* to be showcased on ABC's *Wonderful World of Disney*. "Mostly all-new" would be a more accurate term. The production was to have the same Rodgers and Hammerstein songs (save for a couple of twists), the same basic story (save for a multiracial casting approach), and, most importantly, the same this-is-special-television feel.

Whitney, as executive producer, was assembling an all-name cast befitting the project's sizable (for a TV movie) $12 million budget: Oscar winner Whoopi Goldberg as Prince Charming's mother, Queen Constantina; *Seinfeld*'s Jason Alexander as royal assistant Lionel; and stage and film vet Bernadette Peters (*The Jerk*) as Cinderella's wicked (or, in this toned-down instance, unsympathetic) stepmother. Whitney saved a choice part for herself: the Fairy Godmother.

Then Ms. Houston placed a phone call to Ms. Norwood.

The conversation started as chitchat (as much as a one-on-one with mentor and adoring student can be), with Whitney talking about her daughter. Then she mentioned *Cinderella*. Brandy asked if she could please—*please*—have a little part in the production.

"She said, 'No, I want you to play Cinderella,'" Brandy recalled in *Seventeen*.

Brandy freaked.

"My mom had to pinch me," she later told the audience on *Live! With Regis & Kathie Lee*.

This was called coming full circle to the *fullest* extent—from emulating an idol, to meeting the idol, to appearing on the same album with the idol, to (get this) sharing screen and song time with the idol.

Brandy had become The Anointed One. Handpicked by Whitney Houston herself to be the new Cinderella.

This was going to be *big*.

the big time

Rodgers & Hammerstein's Cinderella was shot on soundstages in Los Angeles during Brandy's downtime between Seasons Three and Four of *Moesha*. Training for the title role meant more than learning how to make a ball gown look good.

Training meant learning to play a character who wasn't a modern-day Los Angeles mallrat, but a Renaissance-era peasant. Training meant learning to sing songs that weren't custom-made grooves, but set-in-stone *song*-songs by a legendary songwriting team.

Brandy, in short, wasn't going to be able to cut it just doing Brandy. She was going to have to *be* Cinderella. She was going to have to compete against every preconceived notion of what a

Cinderella should look and talk and sing like. She was going to have to battle the memories of the 1950 Disney animated feature, of Julie Andrews, of Lesley Ann Warren. This was a part with serious baggage.

Good thing Brandy wasn't afraid of heavy lifting.

She got busy with a vocal coach who taught Brandy, R&B star, to meet Brandy, Broadway-bound singer. Even more so than in other forms, musical-theater singing is musical *acting*—every syllable, every breath, every intonation is key. The words, above all, must be heard. Precisely.

As usual, Brandy was a good student.

"My best friends that are my age, they think I'm singing opera," Brandy told *Time for Kids*.

Still other adjustments needed to be made. Brandy's acting experience was essentially limited to the quick-return sitcom world—rehearse a script, shoot a script (pretty much in order), put the episode in the can. In and out in a week's time.

Even if it was for TV, *Cinderella* was still a movie—and there is *no* instant gratification in moviemaking. No supportive studio audience. No apparent logic (with scenes—even dialogue exchanges—filmed out of order). What there is, is a grind. A demanding, exhaustive grind.

"It was difficult to adjust to all the rehearsing," Brandy said in *Seventeen*. "Just when you thought you had it, you didn't."

Suffice to say, the cast and crew of *Rodgers & Hammerstein's Cinderella* finally got it.

The finished product premiered on ABC on November 2, 1997. As *The New York Times* declared: "The Glass Slipper Fits with a '90s Conscience." Critics took notice of the hard-to-miss story updates (the can-do, self-empowerment talk, the color-blind casting), and they liked them. They liked Brandy, too. "Amazingly good," the *Times* said.

Brandy's high-wire act—daring to boldly go where only a few would-be princesses had gone before—achieved its desired effect.

She had stood her own against the veteran cast. She blossomed in the scenes with Houston. She made a cute couple with Prince Charming, played by Paolo Montalban. She did the Rodgers and Hammerstein tunes justice. She even made the

A dream is a wish your heart makes: Brandy with her fairy godmother, Whitney Houston. (Copyright © 1997 ABC-TV. Supplied by Photofest.)

usually dreaded (by women) blue eye shadow—as donned for the big ballroom dance sequence—look good.

Brandy had accepted the Cinderella challenge and won.

And some sixty million people watched her triumph.

The ratings for *Cinderella* were huge—the highest for ABC in the two-hour, 7 P.M.–9 P.M. Sunday block in fourteen years.

If Brandy was still considered a niche artist—as in *just* a teen singer, or *just* a sitcom star (on UPN, no less)—then her niche had widened considerably after *Cinderella*. Even *grandmas* knew who Brandy was now. She was everywhere.

The TV-movie's monster appeal proved she was a performer whose appeal cut across age, race, and social lines. Granted, she wasn't the only reason people tuned in—Whitney Houston and the other cast members had more than a little to do with that— but by the end of the two hours, Brandy *was* the reason they were still watching and rooting when she got her storybook wedding.

America has a thing for its Cinderellas.

the un–fairy tale

Cinderella got the guy. Brandy, however, lacking her counterpart's neat ability to fade away with happy ending intact, lost *her* guy. First love became first love lost.

Brandy and Wanya were smiling pretty for the press at *Cinderella*'s premiere party in fall 1997, but by early 1998, the party was over.

Brandy didn't go taking out ads to announce the bust-up. She was as circumspect in ex-girlfriend mode as she had been in girlfriend mode. The reasons for the split came out only in dribs and drabs as Brandy shared little stuff with interviewers: they were too busy to maintain the relationship; she was too young for something so serious. Brandy indicated she headed for the exit first, but that fact didn't spare her feelings—"heartbroken" was how she described herself. Oh, she and Wanya would make attempts to keep in touch, to stay friends, but that didn't change what was.

Brandy was on her own.

chapter seven top of the world

"She's grown up, but she's still Brandy."

—*USA Today*

*I*t was going on four years now with still no follow-up to *Brandy* in stores. It wasn't like the record company wasn't asking. It wasn't like the fans weren't waiting. It wasn't like the scene wasn't wondering: what's up with Brandy? Was "Cinderella" too good for the down-and-dirty record biz? Was she retiring or something—never, ever comin' back?

Never say never.

making tracks

"I had to get my confidence up because I had been away so long," Brandy said in *Best of Rap and R&B* magazine.

Hiding in Moesha Mitchell's bedroom, or Cinderella's ball gown, had grown comfortable. *Too* comfortable. She had to get back to being Brandy. *Had to.*

She wasn't the only one feeling the pull, or applying the pressure. Atlantic Records wanted its multiplatinum artist back on the shelves something fierce.

"Janet and Mariah's new records are just a loop of someone else," Atlantic executive vice-president Craig Kallman said in an anticipatory huddle with producers, as reported in *New York* magazine. "I think it's wide open for Brandy to take them out.

"When she starts singing, it's hot. . . ."

That was the key: "When she *starts* singing." When exactly was that going to be? Rumored release dates in 1996 gave way to rumored release dates in 1997 gave way to . . .

Brandy, while copping to a bad case of insecurity, *was* secure in one thing: she wasn't going to sing what she didn't feel. Just as with her debut album, she needed material—the *right* material, the *right* vibe. Brandy was searching, and she seemed to keep coming back to one theme: the new album couldn't be the old album. She wasn't *that* Brandy anymore.

• "I'm not the 'I Wanna Be Down' little girl on a swing. I've grown up," she said to *Billboard* magazine.

• "When I'm eighteen, I should talk about things that eighteen-year-olds talk about," she remarked to the Los Angeles *Daily News.*

Helping Brandy connect with her eighteen-year-old self in mid-1997 was a guy who was all of nineteen himself: Rodney Jerkins.

A fellow prodigy and classically trained musician, Jerkins started turning heads in the music business at age fifteen when his homemade demo tapes attracted professional producing gigs. By the time he turned 1-9, he had worked his "darkchild funk" style—his personal brand of R&B—for Mary J. Blige, Aaliyah, and the Backstreet Boys.

"Because I'm so young, I've got a lot of energy," Jerkins said in *EMI's Songwriter Spotlight.*

Brandy connected with that energy and together the two created the majority of the tracks that would make up that elusive second album.

Chief among their concoctions: "The Boy Is Mine."

Brandy helped Jerkins and three others craft the cool tug-of-war tale. Far from the jokey bantering of 1982's Michael Jackson/Paul McCartney similarly titled hit, "The Girl Is Mine," "The Boy Is Mine" was a calculated, dead-eyed confrontation.

And Brandy knew exactly whom she should square off against on the record: Monica.

the summit

Monica Arnold, born 1980, was yet another of Brandy's too-young, too-blessed contemporaries—arguably, the leading one. In fact, in many ways, Monica was Brandy's mirror image (or, as Brandy has called her, "little sister"). Monica, too, was a product of the South (Atlanta, Georgia, to Brandy's McComb, Mississippi) who sang in church choir, developed a major Whitney Houston hang-up, excelled in school, and released her first album before she was old enough to drive (1995's *Miss Thang,* recorded when she was fourteen for Whitney's longtime label home, Arista Records). They even shared an Usher connection—he contributed vocals to Monica's debut CD.

How to tell them apart? Well, Brandy you believed when she told you she was fifteen; Monica, almost two years her junior, you wanted to card. The difference was a matter of style. *Miss Thang*—from its snap-your-fingers title to its sultry-voiced No. 1 R&B hits, "Don't Take It Personal (Just One of Dem Days)" and "Before You Walk Out of My Life"—was all sassy attitude to *Brandy*'s polite longings.

The early word on these two was that, despite more than a few fundamental similarities, they were oil and water—didn't mix.

"It's ironic that Brandy and I came out at the same time,"

Monica told *Newsweek* in 1998. "We knew the comparisons would be huge, but not all the talk about us being at each other's throats."

Both denied they were waging a Godzilla-esque, Brandy-vs.-Monica war for the right to R&B's young diva crown. Still, the catfight stories persisted.

Then Brandy had an idea.

"We need to do a song together," Brandy told her supposedly embittered rival, as she recalled for *Black Beat*. "It'll shock everybody."

Monica liked the song Brandy and Jerkins had cooked up, but worried that fans would mistake the verbal jousting on "The Boy Is Mine" for further proof of their animosity—maybe even offer extra-suspicious types a smoking gun. ("So, that's why they hate each other! They duked it out over a boy!") The promise of a music video, which, if nothing else, would offer visual evidence that the two could share the same airspace without coming to blows, was the deal-sealer. The video, Monica told *Word Up!*, would show "the song was definitely done in fun."

To prep for their recording date, Brandy went down to Atlanta to hang with Monica. Outsiders expecting Armageddon were disappointed. In Atlanta, Brandy and Monica shopped, talked, took in an amusement park, and peaceably cemented their commitment to the duet. If Brandy wanted an attention-getter for her new album, then Monica certainly could use one for hers, too—her sophomore collection was also in the works. Together, the two had much to gain. *How much* there was to be gained would be very clear by the summer of 1998.

Brandy and Monica first attempted to record the vocals for "The Boy Is Mine" in New York, but the vibe wasn't happening. It would take a second session to get the pulsating standoff down cold—real cold. It was worth the extra effort. Monica's record label ended up borrowing the cut as the title for its star's new album. If that move bothered Brandy (and she said it didn't), she could console herself with the bottom line: Monica's CD sales would mean royalties for Brandy, who had a piece of "The Boy Is Mine" songwriting booty.

Making alliances is always a lot smarter than making enemies.

Miss Thang *herself:* Brandy's *"little sister,"* Monica, at the 12th Annual Soul Train *Music Awards.* (Copyright © 1998 Lisa Rose/ Globe Photos, Inc.)

all-new brandy

"The Boy Is Mine" wasn't the only new cut from the pen of Brandy. She was exerting herself big time as a songwriter on the new project, sharing credit on six of its fourteen tracks. The best way, apparently, to make sure she was covering material that was true to her post-*Brandy* experiences was to supply the material herself.

The new album, to be tagged *Never Say Never,* was replete with themes close to the heart of a young woman who'd enjoyed first love and endured first breakup. "Have You Ever?" (about a sweet romance), the title track (about a more fitful, we-can-make-this-work-if-we-really-try relationship), and "Learn the Hard Way" (about the finality of a busted heart), all effectively mined that territory.

But if you wanted the best example of the difference between old Brandy and new Brandy, it was "Angel in Disguise," the song slotted in the CD's leadoff position. The track saw Brandy playing a two-timed girlfriend who lost her man to an "angel in disguise." More than that, it heard Brandy—little ole Brandy—singing about undeniable "lust."

In the context of, say, the Prince songbook, it was hardly shocking or explicit stuff. In the context of *Cinderella,* it was an eye-opener.

And that was the way Brandy wanted it. This album was her first statement on the record (literally) as an adult. She needed to keep it real, just as she'd kept it real (in a more teenybopper spirit) on *Brandy.* It was time for music's "good girl" to remind people that it was "good *woman*" now. Like the song title said: "U Don't Know Me (Like U Used To)."

"I'm nineteen," Brandy told *Seventeen* in a post-album release interview in 1998. "If I want to have sex, I have every right to."

Her core beliefs were unchanged: marriage first, sex second. Brandy was just making it plain that she deserved credit for being a grown-up. Don't go getting all bent out of shape if she sings the word "lust"—she was still Brandy. She was still the dutiful, live-at-home daughter. She wasn't going to go Marilyn Manson on you. She just wanted the freedom to act her older age.

Mr. "Harlem World": Mase arrives at the 11th Annual Soul Train Music Awards. (Copyright © 1997 Lisa Rose/Globe Photos, Inc.)

Which brings up the subject of Mase.

The Brandy of 1994 or 1995 told interviewers who would listen that she dug gangsta rap—liked the sounds of Tupac and Notorious B.I.G.—but were they listening? The Brandy of 1998 delivered the proof that, as she put it to *Black Beat,* "I'm good-home-training ghetto." Right there on *Never Say Never,* in between R&B grooves like "The Boy Is Mine" and the gospel-tinged "One Voice," was "Top of the World," wherein Brandy Norwood mixed it up with Mr. "Harlem World" himself—Mase.

The former Mason Bertha was born in Florida in 1975, but raised in the Harlem section of New York City—ground zero for Puff Daddy's burgeoning rap empire. Mase's first love was basketball. He snagged a sports scholarship to a New York state university before an injury ended his hoop dreams and prompted his hip-hop career. Mase hooked up with Puff Daddy and became Bad Boy Entertainment's unofficial house rapper, performing on dozens of cuts for everybody from Mariah Carey to B.I.G. In 1997, he got his solo shot on the *Harlem World* collection. Mase wasn't hardcore of the

hardcore, but he wasn't Vanilla Ice, either, as his rap, "The Player Way," would indicate.

Mase first met Brandy at a New York nightclub party when she was dating Wanya. They kept in touch, in part because

Brandy was an unabashed fan. At her urging, he looked into hooking up with her mom's management company and, eventually, signed on. Mase, the rapper, and Brandy, the princess, had the same "Momager." The arrangement sounded good to Brandy.

"It's fun hanging out with Mase," she told *Right On!* "I've lived a sheltered life, so he's showing me new things."

Now, Mase wasn't out to corrupt Brandy. For one thing, he was always checking with her mom to see if things were cool. For another, Brandy *was* Brandy. Consider the time Mase took Brandy to meet fellow rapper Lil' Kim . . . and the music industry power trio ended up chowing down at (where else?) McDonald's.

The duo's friendship—and that's what they both say it is, despite some reported public hand-holding—translated into the collaboration "Top of the World," a seemingly autobiographical cut, with Brandy singing about how people think she lives a fairy tale, and Mase contributing a rap. It was a potent combo. (One they re-created for the *MTV Movie Awards* in June 1998.)

Brandy had started work on *Never Say Never* prior to the *Cinderella* shoot. Once that dream TV-movie came along, she put the album on hold—again. But at least things were headed in the right direction. Hesitations had given way to game plans. The album *was* eventually completed, with finishing touches added after *Cinderella* wrapped. The *Never Say Never* mission was complete. Almost.

Once again, Brandy deployed album cover art to help make her case. Where *Brandy* featured a simple, meet-the-new-kid shot, *Never Say Never* looked like a Calvin Klein ad—mysterious and moody in black-and-white. Cropped to reveal only the right side of her face, the picture was arresting and sophisticated. The contrasts between the album covers were striking—almost as jarring as Monica going from tomboy to glam-girl in the space of *her* two albums. Old Brandy reveled in mallwear; new Brandy, as accompanying pictures in the CD booklet attested, modeled designer wear.

Brandy wasn't showing off—she was just letting on that she wasn't the quiet-looking kid in homeroom anymore. A hit album and a long-running hit TV show had made her more than a peer.

She was a style-setter—the cool upperclassman the other kids secretly yearned to be like. Sure, Brandy could have tried to duck the role—deny that people looked up to her, pretend everything was the same. But that wouldn't have been the truth. That wouldn't have been Brandy.

Make that, the all-new Brandy.

the hit is theirs

The long-awaited *Never Say Never* was released on June 9, 1998. A week later it opened at No. 3 on *Billboard*'s pop album charts. Two months later, its sales topped two million (and counting). No one was more interested in the public response than Brandy. She admitted that she called her label every week to track its performance. The numbers looked good. *Very* good.

"In the end, people want good music," Atlantic Records executive Ron Shapiro said in *Billboard*. And that's what he thought she delivered. An "incredible" record, he said.

Critics generally agreed. *USA Today* awarded the album three-and-three-quarters stars—a notch below a perfect four. *Billboard* found it full of "remarkable maturity . . . replete with potential singles." *Entertainment Weekly* said the all-new Brandy "bursts with enough naive charm to make Jewel look like a jaded sailor."

The first single was the Monica duet. Brandy's notion that the two could shock the world by joining forces had been dead-solid perfect. "The Boy Is Mine" became *the* song of the summer. The thing was *everywhere*—on radio, on MTV, on the charts. It was Brandy's first No. 1 overall pop hit. (Monica's, too.) The two teens got to enjoy the view from the top of the heap for thirteen weeks. Only the Mariah Carey/Boyz II Men coupling on 1995's "One Sweet Day" held the No. 1 spot longer.

Unfortunately, the success didn't stop the rumblings about oil and water. The video didn't change minds, either, even if it depicted Brandy and Monica teaming up to scam the boy who scammed them.

An appearance by Brandy on NBC's *Tonight Show* in May 1998 fueled whispers of an unfriendly rivalry. Brandy performed

"The Boy Is Mine" as a solo—sans Monica. Brandy, though, wasn't trying to dis Monica, the official story said—Monica just couldn't attend the taping because of a scheduling conflict.

It appeared that the backstage intrigue would finally dissolve when the two performed *together* at the 15th Annual *MTV Video Music Awards* on September 10, 1998. Dressed-to-kill in gowns that gave the rocked-out ceremony a touch of class, Brandy and Monica slinked and sashayed and head-bobbed their way through a dramatic, faithful rendition of their hit single. The performance seemed smooth and seamless. They walked onto the stage together. They walked off the stage together. Done deal.

But if Brandy and Monica were hoping the joint appearance would quell the rumors of a blood feud, they underestimated the persistence of backstabbers. A few days after the show, reports circulated that the two had come to blows just prior to the performance.

Never mind that neither Brandy nor Monica went into hiding after the supposed brawl, but instead met with reporters for post-awards coverage. Never mind that Brandy herself turned up days later at the 50th Annual *Primetime Emmy Awards* singing a solo from *Cinderella* and looking entirely *un*punched. No, believers of the rumors had a ready explanation: makeup. One problem: if makeup worked like magic—hiding every line, every wrinkle, every *split lip* (?!?)—Hollywood types wouldn't be shelling out jumbo-sized bucks for face-saving plastic surgery.

Enough was enough. About a week after the MTV Awards, the camps of Brandy and Monica issued a joint statement to set the record straight.

"Over the past three years, some individuals have attempted to paint Brandy and Monica as adversaries," the statement said. "Such ongoing negativity is totally unfair to these two gifted teenagers."

Where the MTV Awards were concerned, the statement said that the two shared adjoining dressing rooms, sat next to each other in the audience, even shared a prayer before their performance.

End of story.

Monica poses with Brandy backstage at the 15th Annual MTV Video Music Awards. *(Copyright © 1998 Fitzroy Barrett/Globe Photos, Inc.)*

Sort of. The statement went on to note that Brandy and Monica were talking about the possibility of doing a joint tour.

That ought to give the world something to talk about.

fright queen

Her recording career set straight, Brandy, in 1998, finally had the time to give movies a real shot again. None of this left-on-the-cutting-room-floor stuff anymore. Brandy was ready for the big-time, big-screen close-up.

She picked a good time to go looking for movie roles. She also picked a good time to be nineteen, which she was, as of February. The box-office success of 1996's *Scream*, starring Neve Campbell and Drew Barrymore, reinvented that most resilient of genres: the teen horror flick. Back in the day, these movies weren't pretty—usually no more than low-budget productions packed with heavy petting and buckets of blood (the better to sell tickets)—but they *were* an employment boon to young, nubile actors who were willing to get carved, chased, and slashed for the pleasure of directors and audiences. The movies made household names of Freddy Krueger, Michael Meyers, and Jason Voorhees—the psycho killers of, respectively, the *Nightmare on Elm Street, Halloween,* and *Friday the 13th* franchises. *Scream* took the genre into the 1990s—self-consciously acknowledging its debt to Freddy and friends, upping the hip factor in the dialogue department, and quickening the pace, while flashing the requisite knives.

I Know What You Did Last Summer, released in 1997, was one of the teens-in-peril movies (*Disturbing Behavior, Urban Legends,* and *Halloween H²0* were others) rushed into theaters in search of the *Scream* audience. *I Know . . .* had better genes than most for the assignment. Based on a young-adult horror novel by author Lois Duncan, its script was by Kevin Williamson, the guy who wrote the trendsetting *Scream* and, later, the equally famous *Scream 2.* (He's also responsible for the WB's teens-in-angst drama series, *Dawson's Creek.*) The movie told the story of four friends (including TV's *Buffy, the Vampire Slayer,* Sarah Michelle Geller) who accidentally kill a dude, and the dude who comes back to skewer them with his nifty fishhook hand for revenge. It wasn't as clever or fresh as *Scream,* but it worked—and it made bank, earning more than $72 million at the box office. You didn't need to be a card-carrying studio mogul to know what was coming next: a sequel.

Just so no one missed the point (HEY, IT'S A SEQUEL!), the project was unabashedly dubbed *I Still Know What You Did Last Summer.* Jennifer Love Hewitt, the *Party of Five* star who managed to avoid the fishhook in the first film, was set to return as good-girl Julie James. So was Freddie Prinze Jr., who played her sensitive high-school love, Ray Bronson. The rest of the casting slate was pretty much open—just about all the other characters Julie and Ray hung with in *I Know* . . . didn't make it out alive. Producers needed fresh meat. (Figuratively speaking.)

Brandy was more than willing to volunteer. She told her agent that she'd love a part in the new movie. Horror flicks, it seemed, were her kind of thing.

"I love, love, love being scared," she said, by way of explanation, in the *New York Daily News.*

Brandy got her wish. And a pretty cool role, too.

She was cast as Hewitt's new best friend, Karla Wilson. The character wasn't Moesha Mitchell. She wasn't Cinderella. She wasn't Brandy. She was, rather, "a hot mama, a real fast girl," Brandy offered to *Best of Rap and R&B* magazine. All that, plus Karla worked in a bar. Fine by Brandy. It was good to try on somebody else's life for a while or, in the case of the *I Still Know* . . . production, for a summer.

Shooting got under way in summer 1998 in Mexico (standing in for the Bahamas), south of the resort area of Puerto Vallarta. Also joining the cast were new face Matthew Settle as Prinze's romantic rival, Will Benson, and Mekhi Phifer as Tyrell Martin, Brandy's romantic interest. Phifer was a definite old face to Brandy—he played the no-good boy in the video for "The Boy Is Mine."

For this band of young actors, the pressure was on. Even before a scene was in the can, a November 20, 1998, release date had been set. Sony Pictures was banking on *I Still Know* . . . to be its big-ticket Thanksgiving Day-weekend draw. By far, the biggest

challenge facing the film was how to manage success minus any Kevin Williamson-supplied plot twists. The *Scream*-meister was too busy making his own teens-in-peril opus, *Killing Mrs. Tingle*, to deal with the *I Know . . .* franchise. Enlisted to dream up new mayhem for Julie James was newcomer Trey Callaway. His script picked up one year after the close of *I Know . . .* and found Hewitt's character jumpy and still kind of freaked by the events of the first film. To the rescue: best bud Karla, who prescribes a vacation to the Bahamas for the girls and their respective guys.

"There's a lot more action this time, a lot more energy," director Danny Cannon (*Judge Dredd*) told *Entertainment Weekly.* "And a great exotic location."

About that location: the steamy south-of-the-border shoot represented a big move—geographically and personally—for Brandy. She might have toured the world as a performer, but she'd almost always had her "Momager" with her. Not this time. She was on her own. At night, it was just her . . . and all those weird critters (red ants, scorpions, beetles, lizards, etc.) that regularly invaded the hotel and set.

"I brought a big bottle of Raid," Brandy said in *Premiere* magazine. "I am prepared."

And she was. She handled life (which now included kickboxing training) on her own on a faraway movie set okay. *More* than okay.

"I'm the happiest I've ever been," she told columnists Marilyn Beck and Stacy Jenel Smith. "I love doing a lot of physical stuff as I am in this movie . . . I love running from the killer!"

As for seeing the finished product? Actually seeing herself—twenty feet high on a movie screen—getting chased around by a crazy fishhook guy?

"It will be so weird watching myself . . . and thinking, 'Any minute now I could be dead,'" she said in the *New York Daily News.* "It's so fun—as long as it's not for real."

What was real was *this:* Brandy was about to blow up as a *movie star.*

Music star. TV star. Movie star.

She'd aced them all.

At age nineteen.

Was there anything left?
You bet.

postscript

There was so much she still wanted to do, Brandy once said. So much she still wanted to accomplish.

Like what?

It was late 1998. Wasn't she back at work on a fourth season of *Moesha*? Wasn't her name up in lights on movie marquees, trumpeting her co-starring role in *I Still Know What You Did Last Summer*? Wasn't *Never Say Never* still ringing up CD sales?

Wasn't there talk of tours, of collaborations with Sean "Puffy" Combs, of new movie projects?

Wasn't there a new TV and film production company that her mom was setting up? Wasn't there a chance for her to play executive producer on a new TV-movie to star Ray J?

Wasn't she Cover Girl's newest spokesmodel, right up there in TV commercials with Tyra Banks? Wasn't she the youngest endorser for Candie's shoes, posing for ads with the likes of Li'l Kim and Shania Twain? Wasn't she hooked up with the prestigious Wilhelmina modeling agency, right alongside her Atlantic Records label mates Duncan Sheik ("Barely Breathing") and Li'l Kim (again)?

Well, yeah, Brandy was all that.

But why stop there?

She wanted to resume college. (Something had had to give in her packed schedule and, unfortunately, that had been school time.) She wanted to meet a "dime" (a.k.a., the "perfect gentleman"). She wanted to have kids one day, and to raise those kids in the church.

She wanted more. She wanted better.

Achieving your dream doesn't mean much if you don't make the most of the dream. Take advantage of the view. Play the table.

Brandy was making the most of it.

From McComb to Carson to Hollywood to beyond—she'd passed every test. Exceeded every expectation. And, maybe even harder, lived up to every expectation.

It's hard growing up. It's hard growing up when the whole world's watching—and the whole world's thinking you've got to do it ten-point-oh perfect.

Brandy made it look easy. She tapped into a talent, set a goal, got to work. No secret formula. No fairy godmother required.

Brandy Norwood wasn't touched by magic.

She *made* her own magic.

Looking to the future: Brandy poses on the set of Moesha. (Copyright © 1998 UPN. Supplied by Globe Photos, Inc.)

brandy f.y.i.

Name: Brandy Rayana Norwood

Claims to fame: Singer, actress, model, role model

Birth date: February 11, 1979

Birthplace: McComb, Mississippi

Height: 5'7"

Family: Mom: Sonja Norwood; Dad: Willie Ray Norwood, Sr.; younger brother: Willie Ray Norwood, Jr. (Ray J)

Astrological sign: Aquarius

Personal status: Single (no steady)

Current residence: Lives with her family in Southern California's San Fernando Valley

Education: Enrolled at Pepperdine University in Malibu, California

Wheels: A Lexus GS400 and a Range Rover

Favorite fashions: Tommy Hilfiger, Donna Karan, Ralph Lauren

Favorite musical artists: Boyz II Men, Mariah Carey, Celine Dion, Whitney Houston, Mase, Alanis Morissette, Notorious B.I.G., Puff Daddy, Tupac Shakur

Favorite school subjects: Drama, English, Music, Psychology

Favorite sport: Basketball

Favorite TV shows: Beavis & Butt-head, The Cosby Show, Step by Step, Full House

Guilty pleasures: McDonald's french fries and cheeseburgers

Official fan club: The Brandy International Fan Club
15030 Ventura Blvd. #710
Sherman Oaks, CA 91403

Okay, you've read this book—but have you *read* this book? Time to see who's paying attention and who's waiting for the movie adaptation:

Easy-Breezy

1. Which sitcom marked Brandy's debut as a series regular?
   (a) *The Cosby Show*
   (b) *Moesha*
   (c) *Thea*

2. Brandy went to a high-school prom with which current NBA star?
   (a) Kobe Bryant
   (b) Kevin Garnett
   (c) Keith Van Horn

3. The song "Best Friend," from the *Brandy* album, is about which VIP in the singer's life?
   (a) Her brother, Ray J
   (b) Her *Moesha* costar, Countess Vaughn
   (c) Her mother, Sonja

4. Which rising music star played Brandy's TV boyfriend Jeremy on *Moesha*?
   (a) Isaac Hanson
   (b) Mase
   (c) Usher

5. The 1997 TV movie *Rodgers & Hammerstein's Cinderella* was watched by how many million people?
   (a) 25
   (b) 60
   (c) 85

So-So

6. At age fourteen, this label signed Brandy to a record contract:
   (a) Atlantic
   (b) Capitol
   (c) Motown

7. On which movie soundtrack does a Brandy track not appear?
   (a) *Batman Forever*
   (b) *The English Patient*
   (c) *Set It Off*

8. Why did Brandy perform "The Boy Is Mine" sans duet partner Monica on *The Tonight Show*?
   (a) Brandy hates Monica
   (b) Monica hates Brandy
   (c) They like each other just fine. A scheduling conflict prevented Monica from attending the taping.

9. Which award-show honor has Brandy not captured (yet)?
   (a) The American Music Award
   (b) The Grammy
   (c) The MTV Movie Award

10. How many million records did Brandy's self-titled debut album, *Brandy*, sell?
    (a) 4
    (b) 5
    (c) 6

Getting Tougher

11. In which year did *Moesha* premiere?
    (a) 1994

(b) 1995

(c) 1996

12. For the movie shoot of *I Still Know What You Did Last Summer*, Brandy spent much of her last summer holed up in which country?
    (a) Canada
    (b) Cuba
    (c) Mexico

13. When Whitney Houston telephones Brandy at home, the teen singer says she:
    (a) Puts *The Bodyguard* star on call waiting
    (b) Records their conversations
    (c) Screams

14. Brandy is the youngest celebrity endorser for which shoe company?
    (a) Candie's
    (b) Hush Puppies
    (c) Nike

15. The ballad "(Everything I Do) I Do It for You," from the *Never Say Never* album, was originally recorded by which rocker?
    (a) Bryan Adams
    (b) Lou Reed
    (c) Bruce Springsteen

Ph.D. Required

16. In which college did Brandy enroll in 1996?
    (a) California State University, Northridge
    (b) Pepperdine University
    (c) University of Southern California

17. Also in 1996, Brandy appeared as a special guest on what legendary pop crooner's network TV special?
    (a) Tony Bennett
    (b) Jack Jones
    (c) Frank Sinatra

18. Brandy has a one-inch scar located on a(n):
    (a) elbow
    (b) foot
    (c) knee

19. If Brandy's got a craving for fast food, which fine-dining establishment is she most likely to do a drive-through drop-in on?
    (a) Burger King
    (b) McDonald's
    (c) El Pollo Loco

20. How many years were there between the releases of *Brandy* and *Never Say Never*?
    (a) 2
    (b) 3
    (c) 4

Answers

1. (c) 2. (a) 3. (a) 4. (c) 5. (b) 6. (a)
7. (b) 8. (c) 9. (b) 10. (a) 11. (c)
12. (c) 13. (c) 14. (a) 15. (a) 16. (b)
17. (a) 18. (a) 19. (b) 20. (c)

Scoring

18–20: EXPERT. Geez, maybe it's time to move onto another singer or something because you—you Brandyphile, you—have got Brandy down cold. Congratulations. And try not to brag.

12–17: SCHOLAR. You demonstrate a solid knowledge of all things Brandy. There are a few gaps in your understanding, yes, but that's okay. Maybe you're the type who prefers listening to the albums rather than dissecting them.

6–11: UNDERGRAD. You've got room to grow. You know the Brandy basics, i.e., you can pick out the hits on the radio, remember what time *Moesha*'s on—stuff like that. But as far as Trivial Pursuit goes? That's not your game.

0–5: NOVICE. Hey, everybody's got to start somewhere, right? Even Brandy.

TV's *Cinderella* princess isn't likely to be confused with a *Melrose Place* drama queen anytime this century. But the lady *does* have her guys. Some are professional entanglements, some friends, and, yes, some romantic hopefuls. With a nod to her No. 1 hit with Monica, here's the lowdown on the boys — in alphabetical order — who are unmistakably hers.

KOBE BRYANT

Claim to fame: The high-school kid who skipped college and jumped right into the NBA as shooting guard for the Los Angeles Lakers.

Birth date: August 23, 1978

Birthplace: Philadelphia, Pennsylvania

Astrological sign: Virgo

Random factoid: Fluent in Italian

Brandy connection: In 1996, he escorted Ms. Norwood on her first date — to his senior prom.

Current status: Sorry, hopeless romantics who think this prodigious duo are a match made for an oh-so-cute profile on a Barbara Walters TV special — they're just "very good friends."

For the record: "I'm so proud of him." — Brandy, in *Ebony*

Kobe Bryant

MASE (MASON BETHA)

Claim to fame: Prolific rapper on Puff Daddy's Bad Boy label

Birth date: August 27, 1975

Birthplace: Jacksonville, Florida

Astrological sign: Virgo

Random factoid: Released his first solo album, *Harlem World*, in 1997

Mase

For the record: "You are honest and sincere and I appreciate you being there for me when I need you." — Brandy, in the *Never Say Never* liner notes

WANYA MORRIS

Claim to fame: Member of the best-selling R&B foursome Boyz II Men ("End of the Road")
Birth date: July 29, 1973
Birthplace: Philadelphia, Pennsylvania
Astrological sign: Leo

Wanya Morris

Brandy connection: Her mom, Sonja, doubles as his manager. Together, they teamed for "Top of the World" on the *Never Say Never* album and performed the cut on the 1998 *MTV Movie Awards.*
Current status: Well, Brandy is a big fan, but they're not dating. However, if things work out, watch for them to grow closer . . . as actors. Mase was in talks to join the cast of *Moesha.*

Random factoid: Stage nickname is "Squirt"

Brandy connection: She toured with Boyz II Men in 1995 and developed a crush on Wanya. Later that year the two recorded a duet—a remake of Brandy's "Brokenhearted"—for a BIIM remix album. While stars were in Brandy's eyes, dating was off-limits until she was safely eighteen. When the birthday arrived, in 1997, Wanya was there.

Current status: It's over (as of early 1998).

For the record: "At nineteen, I don't think it's cool to be all wrapped up in just one guy."—Brandy, in *Seventeen*

Ray J

RAY J (WILLIE RAY NORWOOD, JR.)

Claim to fame: Singer ("Everything You Want"), actor (*Steel*)

Birth date: January 17, 1981

Birthplace: McComb, Mississippi

Astrological sign: Capricorn

Random factoid: Has appeared in commercials for Denny's and McDonald's

Brandy connection: They're brother and sister

Current status: They're still brother and sister—and each other's biggest fans.

For the record: "We help each other. [Ray J is] my best friend."—Brandy, in *People*

Mekhi Phifer

MEKHI PHIFER

Claim to fame: The object of Brandy's and Monica's affection-turned-annoyance in "The Boy Is Mine" video.
Birth year: 1975
Birthplace: New York City, New York
Random factoid: Cast in Spike Lee's 1995 drama *Clockers* after he showed up for an open-call audition. It was his first big break.
Brandy connection: In addition to "The Boy Is Mine," Phifer co-stars with her in the upcoming *I Still Know What You Did Last Summer.*
Current status: More of the same. Phifer may next move onto *Moesha,* where he was reportedly in talks to play a teacher at Moesha's school.

USHER (USHER RAYMOND)

Claim to fame: Often-shirtless R&B singing star ("My Way") who dabbles in acting (*The Faculty*) and modeling (Tommy Hilfiger).
Birth date: October 14, 1978
Hometown: Chattanooga, Tennessee
Astrological sign: Libra
Random factoid: In 1998, signed on for a stint on the CBS-TV soap opera *The Bold and the Beautiful.*
Brandy connection: Played Moesha's clean-cut boyfriend Jeremy on *Moesha*
Current status: Same as always—strictly professional. They both deny whispers of romance. (He's reportedly too busy for any love matches right now.)
For the record: "The guy who gets Brandy will be a lucky one, because she's fine."—Usher, in *Black Beat's Ultimate Usher*

Usher

SEAN "PUFFY" COMBS (a.k.a. PUFF DADDY)

Claim to fame: Enterprising rap mogul (founder of Bad Boy Entertainment); best-selling performer (1997's *No Way Out*).

Birth date: November 4, 1970
Birthplace: Harlem, New York
Astrological sign: Scorpio
Random factoids: Named a Manhattan restaurant in honor of his eldest son, Justin. Named his youngest son, Christopher, after slain rapper friend, the Notorious B.I.G. (real name: Christopher Wallace).
Brandy connection: A tangential one— at best. Mase raps for Combs' Bad Boy label; Brandy's mother manages Mase's career. That's it, really, although Brandy has been known to gush to reporters—even to *The Tonight Show*'s Jay Leno—about how she thinks Puff Daddy is pretty together. However, there *has* been talk of a possible musical collaboration.
Current status: Strictly an unrequited crush/professional admiration thing. Combs is settled with longtime girlfriend Kim Porter, mother of Christopher.

Sean "Puffy" Combs

the brandy look

So, you want to look like Brandy. You think she's, well, kind of cool and, hey, it couldn't hurt to channel a bit of that magic. Not a bad plan. Just understand that, like most things, it's not a simple matter. There's no finger-snapping and—*poof!*—you're Brandy. Hey, even Brandy's got to put in an effort to look like Brandy.

Here's a rundown of some of the essentials of The Brandy Look (in convenient alphabetical order):

Braids

According to an account Brandy once shared with *Seventeen,* she spotted her future trademark hairstyle on a fellow diner at a McDonald's. From there she tracked down the stylist, and the rest is hair history.

While braids are an easy 'do to maintain, they're not an easy 'do to *get*. Brandy's original braiding sessions took eight hours, and they were done every two weeks. Often the braids are a mix of Brandy's real hair and synthetic strands. If you want to try this hair-raising procedure at home, *Teen People* suggests the Finale Braid Sealer gadget for sealing off the braids.

Charles David

Brandy once cited this clothing chain as one of her favorites.

Donna Karan

When Brandy's in her best-dressed mode, this is one of the designers she looks to.

Exercise

Toning exercises like sit-ups help Brandy keep her french fries intake in check.

Ivory Soap

Sometimes Brandy's skin-care regimen has been as simple as this—a nightly dip in the soapsuds.

K.I.S.S.

Keep It Simple, Stupid. It's advice that can work wonders in almost all areas of your life, including fashion. Brandy adheres to moderation even when she's at the flashiest of events. (Witness her smart black gown at the 1998 *MTV Video Music Awards*.) It's no wonder *People* magazine lauded her sense of style as "not overdone."

Lipstick

Brandy favors natural lip colors. Nothing gaudy.

Makeup

Simple. Clean. And, due to a recent endorsement deal, we're betting Cover Girl.

Rampage

One of Brandy's favorite mall shops.

Shoes

For casual outings, we're betting Brandy might recommend Candie's—owing to her recent endorsement deal.

Tommy Hilfiger

One of Brandy's favorite sportswear designers.

Vitamins

Brandy's been known to pop a women's multivitamin to get her daily requirements.

Water

Drink it. Brandy once remarked that she was particularly happy with a magazine photo shoot because her skin looked good. And why did it look good? Because she'd been drinking her water.

ZZZZZ

Get sleep.

discography

SOLO ALBUMS

Brandy (Atlantic Records)
- Release: September 1994
- Key tracks: "Baby," "Brokenhearted," "I Wanna Be Down"

1. "Movin' On"
2. "Baby"
3. "Best Friend"
4. "I Wanna Be Down"
5. "I Dedicate (Part I)"
6. "Brokenhearted"
7. "I'm Yours"
8. "Sunny Day"
9. "As Long As You're Here"
10. "Always on My Mind"
11. "I Dedicate (Part II)"
12. "Love Is on My Side"
13. "Give Me You"
14. "I Dedicate (Part III)"

Never Say Never (Atlantic Records)
- Release: June 1998
- Key tracks: "The Boy Is Mine," "Never Say Never," "Top of the World"

1. "Intro"
2. "Angel in Disguise"
3. "The Boy Is Mine" (with Monica)
4. "Learn the Hard Way"
5. "Almost Doesn't Count"
6. "Top of the World" (featuring Mase)
7. "U Don't Know Me (Like U Used To)"
8. "Never Say Never"
9. "Truthfully"
10. "Have You Ever?"
11. "Put That on Everything"
12. "In the Car Interlude"
13. "Happy"
14. "One Voice"
15. "Tomorrow"
16. "(Everything I Do) I Do It for You"

SOUNDTRACKS

Batman Forever (Atlantic)
- Release: June 1995
- Brandy track: "Where Are You Now?"

Waiting to Exhale (Arista)
- Release: November 1995
- Brandy track: "Sittin' Up in My Room"

Set It Off (Elektra)
- Release: September 1996
- Brandy track: "Missing You" (with Tamia, Gladys Knight, Chaka Khan)

All That (TV show) (RCA)
- Release: November 1996
- Brandy track: "Baby"

OTHER

MTV: Party to Go—Volume 7
    (Tommy Boy)
- Release: October 1995
- Brandy track: "I Wanna Be Down"
(Human Rhythm Hip-Hop Remix,
with Yo-Yo, M. C. Lyte, and
Queen Latifah)

The Remix Collection, Boyz II Men
    (Motown)
- Release: November 1995
- Brandy track: "Brokenhearted" (with
Wanya Morris)

Q's Jook Joint, Quincy Jones
    (Warner Bros.)
- Release: November 1995
- Brandy track: "Rock With You"

1996 Grammy Nominees (Sony)
- Release: February 1996
- Brandy track: "Baby"

MTV: Party to Go—Volume 9 (Tommy
    Boy)
- Release: July 1996
- Brandy track: "Baby" (extended LP
mix)

*Smooth Luv: The Ultimate R&B Songs
    Collection* (Capitol)
- Release: November 1996
- Brandy track: "I Wanna Be Down"

Everything You Want, Ray J (Elektra)
- Release: March 1997
- Brandy track: "Thank You" (with
Ray J)

Maximum R&B (Elektra)
- Release: August 1997
- Brandy track: "I Wanna Be Down"
(Human Rhythm Hip-Hop Remix,
with Yo-Yo, M. C. Lyte, and Queen
Latifah)

*Atlantic Records 50 Years:
    Gold Anniversary Collection*
    (Atlantic Records)
- Release: March 1998
- Brandy track: "Baby"

brandy tv/film credits

FILM

Arachnophobia (Disney)
- Release: 1990
- Role: Brandy Beechwood
- Key co-stars: Jeff Daniels (*Dumb and Dumber*), John Goodman (*Roseanne*)
- The scoop: This scary-fun tale of a small town besieged by killer spiders marks the film debut of Brandy, age eleven. It's a blink-and-you-missed-it part—and, in fact, we did. Good luck hunting.

I Still Know What You Did Last Summer (Sony)
- Release: November 1998
- Role: Karla Wilson
- Key co-stars: Jennifer Love Hewitt (*Party of Five*), Mekhi Phifer ("The Boy Is Mine" video)
- The scoop: Mum's the word on Brandy's big-screen blowout—a top-billed outing as Hewitt's college roommate in this anticipated sequel to 1997's teen-scream demi-classic *I Know What You Did Last Summer*. Curious? All will be revealed by Thanksgiving.
- For the record: ". . . I'll tell you one thing, the sequel will be more intense than the original." —Brandy, in *HX* magazine

TV SERIES

Thea (ABC-TV)
- Premiere: September 8, 1993
- Last show: February 23, 1994
- Role: Danesha Turrell
- Key co-star: comedienne Thea Vidale
- The scoop: Fourteen-year-old Brandy plays Vidale's thirteen-year-old daughter in this short-lived comedy series about a widowed mother of four. Look for re-runs to pop up on cable's Black Entertainment Television (BET).
- For the record: "I grew up a lot [making this series]. I learned the responsibilities of having a job." —Brandy, in *Best of Rap and R&B* magazine

Moesha (UPN)
- Premiere: January 23, 1996
- Role: Moesha Mitchell
- Key co-stars/guest stars: Countess Vaughn, Usher, Andrew Keegan (*7th Heaven*)
- The scoop: Already a certified pop star, Brandy, age fifteen, becomes a certified TV star with this peppy, positive sitcom about an impeccably clothed teen, her dad (William Allen Young), stepmom (Sheryl Lee Ralph), and precocious younger brother (Marcus T. Paulk).

• For the record: "[Brandy] brings complete legitimacy to the part of a teenager."—*Moesha* creator Ralph Farquhar, in *People*

TV-MOVIE

Rodgers & Hammerstein's Cinderella (ABC-TV)

• Premiere: November 2, 1997
• Role: Cinderella
• Key co-stars: Whitney Houston (*Waiting to Exhale*), Whoopi Goldberg (*How Stella Got Her Groove Back*), Jason Alexander (*Seinfeld*)
• The scoop: Winning musical remake of oft-told glass-slipper tale. Brandy goes coast to coast big-time as sixty million people catch some, or all, of the broadcast. Now available on home video.
• For the record: "Brandy is amazingly good."—Caryn James, *The New York Times*

VIDEO

Brandy

• Release: 1995
• The scoop: Released in conjunction with self-titled album of same name.

OTHER

Hollywood Lives (Disney Channel)

• Premiere: August 3, 1995
• The scoop: A ten-part documentary series about the lives of young showbiz hopefuls, including one Miss Brandy Norwood.

Tony Bennett: Here's to the Ladies (CBS-TV)

• Premiere: Fall 1996
• The scoop: Veteran pop crooner ("I Left My Heart in San Francisco") pays tribute to female performers and schmoozes with guests stars the likes of Liza Minnelli, Patti LaBelle, and, yes, Brandy.

Ray J in Concert with Brandy (Disney Channel)

• Premiere: September 26, 1997
• The scoop: Sibling revelry is on display in this special spotlighting Brandy's younger brother.

Spice Girls: Too Much is Never Enough (UPN)

• Premiere: December 2, 1997
• The scoop: Brandy hosts the U.S. prime time debut of Britain's wannabe pop sensations in this hour-long special, mixing interviews and music footage.

awards! awards! awards!

Brandy's a collector: hit singles, straight-A report cards, and awards. *Lots* of awards. Here's a sampling of some of the shiny paperweights and other cool honors that Brandy has collected . . . so far.

1990

Named: Darling of the Brotherhood Crusade, Los Angeles, California

1995

Billboard Video Music Award — Rap, Best New Artist Clip: ''I Wanna Be Down (Remix)''

Billboard Video Music Award — R&B/Urban, Best New Clip: ''Baby''

BMI Pop Awards: "Baby"

Named: Spokeswoman, Sears/*Seventeen* Peak Performance Scholarship Program and Tour

Soul Train Lady of Soul Award — Best R&B/Soul Single: "I Wanna Be Down" (from *Brandy*)

Soul Train Lady of Soul Award — Best R&B/Soul Album of the Year, Solo: *Brandy*

Soul Train Lady of Soul Award —

R&B/Soul Song of the Year: "I Wanna Be Down" (from *Brandy*)

Soul Train Lady of Soul Award: Best R&B/Soul New Artist (for *Brandy*)

1996

American Music Award: Favorite New Artist, Soul/R&B

MTV Movie Award — Best Song: "Sittin' Up in My Room" (from *Waiting to Exhale*)

NAACP Image Award: Best New Artist (for Brandy)

Named: "50 Most Beautiful People," *People* magazine

Named: "10 Best Dressed," *People* magazine

Nickelodeon's Kids' Choice Award: Favorite Singer

Soul Train Lady of Soul Award: Entertainer of the Year

1997

NAACP Image Award: Best Youth Actor (for *Moesha*)

1998

Named: "10 Best Dressed," *People* magazine

cyber brandy

Is there any corner of the universe where Brandy's reach does *not* extend? Of course not. The multimedia star is appropriately well-represented on the World Wide Web. Here's a sampling of sites chock-full of factoids, pictures, audio clips, and assorted Brandy-rific stuff.

OFFICIAL

Atlantic Records
http://www.atlantic-records.com/

A somewhat complicated-to-navigate site, but if you want the real deal from Brandy's record label, this is the place. Biography, audio clips, and tour info.

Brandy Forever
http://www.foreverbrandy.com

The *bomb*, from Brandy's camp its very own self. To get in you'll need to download Shockwave (a program that helps your computer process visuals), but just follow the instructions—it's not so tough. Once inside, get treated to a little Brandy show, complete with music. Pretty cool.

I Still Know What You Did Last Summer
http://www.istillknow.com/

The official site for the Sony Pictures' thriller, opening in theaters November 20, 1998. Review the cast list (featuring, yes, Brandy!), download the trailer, try to imagine the rest of the film.

UPN
http://www.upn.com/home.html

What time is *Moesha* on again? Check it out on the homepage for the United Paramount Network. *Moesha*-specific stuff includes cast list and photo.

FAN

Angel in Disguise: Brandy
http://members.aol.com/aquarium2c/

Pretty design, perfunctory stuff: *Never Say Never* album lyrics, and a modest photo gallery included.

BrandyLand
http://www.geocities.com/~brandylands/

Well-organized, well-maintained site. Tons o' pictures. Don't miss the cute one of Brandy modeling Kobe Bryant's Los Angeles Lakers jersey. All this, plus (why not?) a link to a fan site for Nancy McKeon, the actress who played Jo on *The Facts of Life*.

Brandy Theater
http://www.geocities.com/SunsetStrip/Arena/2918/

Solid news section, with rumor/spoiler info on *I Still Know What You Did Last Summer*. Get interactive: post your own review of *Never Say Never*!

Brandy's Place

http://www.und.ida.liu.se/~andwa984/musik/brandy.html

Very complete. A killer news section that's dutifully updated. An exhaustive collection of audio clips from Brandy's two albums. A work-in-progress Brandy fiction story, drafted by Netizens. An autographed Brandy glossy addressed to the site keeper.

Cinderella Movie Page

http://www.geocities.com/SouthBeach/Shores/7574/Cindmain.html

Modest site maintained by a fan of the 1997 TV-movie. With pictures and song lyrics.

Dianna's Brandy Site

http://www.angelfire.com/hi/thebrandysite/index.html

A picture, a biography. That's about it. Appears to be a work-in-progress.

The Unofficial Brandy Site

http://www.brandy-fan.com/html/links.html

Fairly complete with news and links. What's your favorite song from *Never Say Never*? Participate in a Brandy survey.

OTHER

CelebSite

http://www.celebsite.com/people/brandy/

Brandy stats, reviews of other sites, links to Brandy-related news stories on the *Mr. Showbiz* site.

City of Carson, California

http://www.gjw.com/Fans/Brandy.htm

A tribute from Brandy's adopted hometown. And, if you go back to the main page, you can learn about the community where Brandy spent her formative years.

E! Online — Fact Sheet

http://www.eonline.com/Facts/People/0,12,49589,00.html

Biography, filmography, links to Brandy-related news articles.

SonicNet

http://www.sonicnet.com/artists/artist_frame.jhtml?source=guide&id=678

Biography, album reviews.

Wall of Sound

http://www.wallofsound.com/artists/brandy/

Well-written biography, album reviews, links to Brandy-related news stories.

how to get busy like brandy

One of the things that makes Brandy special is the things she holds as special. As much as her film/TV/singing careers pack her schedule, Brandy finds time to give back, and so can you.

Now, Brandy may have established her own Norwood Kids Foundation to help spread the word, but there's no law that says you're required to mount anything as fancy. The key is getting *involved*—in your school, in your church, in your hometown.

For some ideas on where to start, here are a few groups that Brandy's name has been linked to over the years:

LIFEBeat

What is it? A nonprofit organization sponsored by the music industry to provide services and support for people afflicted with HIV/AIDS.

Contact info: 72 Spring Street, Suite 1103, New York, NY 10012
E-mail: lbeat@aol.com

The National Council of Negro Women, Inc.

What is it? A nonprofit organization, founded in 1935, dedicated to improving the lives of black women, their families and communities. Since 1986, the group has hosted annual Black Family Reunion celebrations across the nation.

Contact info: 633 Pennsylvania Avenue NW, Washington, DC 20004
E-mail: info@ncnw.com (general info); bfr@ncnw.com (Black Family Reunion info)
Website: http://www.ncnw.com

RAINN

What is it? The Rape, Abuse, and Incest National Network—a nonprofit organization devoted to helping victims of sexual assault.

Contact info: 635B Pennsylvania Avenue SE, Washington, DC 20003
E-mail: rainnmail@aol.com
Website: http://www.rainn.org

ABOUT THE AUTHOR

New York-based author Joal Ryan is an award-winning journalist whose feature articles on pop culture, television, and film have appeared in *Swing*, the *Los Angeles Times*, *American Journalism Review*, *Sci-Fi Universe*, and *Film Threat*.

PHOTO CREDITS FOR PAGES 125–138

What's Your Brandy I. Q.? Page 125: Photograph of Brandy and Whitney Houston from *Rodgers & Hammerstein's Cinderella* Copyright © 1997 ABC-TV. Supplied by Globe Photos, Inc.

The Men in Brandy's Life Page 126: Photograph of Brandy and Kobe Bryant at the premiere of Eraser Copyright © 1996 Lisa Rose/Globe Photos, Inc. • Page 127: Photograph of Mase at the 1998 World Music Awards Copyright © 1998 Steve Finn/Globe Photos, Inc.; Photograph of Brandy and Wanya Morris Copyright © 1996 Fitzroy Barrett/Globe Photos, Inc. • Page 128: Photograph of Ray J at the 24th Annual American Music Awards Copyright © 1997 Lisa Rose/Globe Photos, Inc.; Photograph of Mekhi Phifer at the premiere of *The Player's Club* Copyright © 1998 Lisa Rose/Globe Photos, Inc. • Page 129: Photograph of Usher at the 1997 Billboard Music Awards Copyright © 1997 Fitzroy Barrett/Globe Photos, Inc. • Page 130: Photograph of Sean "Puffy" Combs at the 1997 *MTV Movie Awards* Copyright © 1997 Lisa Rose/Globe Photos, Inc.

The Brandy Look Page 131: Photograph of Brandy at a Spring 1996 fashion show Copyright © 1995 Henry McGee/Globe Photos, Inc. • Page 132: Photograph of Brandy at the 1996 Grammy party at Jimmy's Copyright © 1996 Nina Prommer/Globe Photos, Inc. • Page 133: Photograph of Brandy at a UPN affiliates gathering Copyright © 1997 Lisa Rose/Globe Photos, Inc.

Awards! Awards! Awards! Page 138: Photograph of Brandy at the 1996 American Music Awards Copyright © 1996 Lisa Rose/Globe Photos, Inc.

CHAPTER ONE. Weeks, Janet. "Brandy's Big Moment." *TV Guide*, Issue #2364, July 18, 1998, p. 15. Helligar, Jeremy. "Starry-Eyed." *People*, 1998. (Retrieved on-line.) Mr. *Showbiz* (uncredited). "Brandy: The Mr. *Showbiz* Interview." (Retrieved on-line.) Wilbekin, Emil. "16 Candles." *Vibe*, May 1995. (Retrieved on-line.) Lima, O.J. "Cinderella Has Left the Building." *Seventeen*, September 1998, pp. 258–261. Helligar, Jeremy. "Starry-Eyed." *People*, 1998. (Retrieved on-line.) Wilbekin, Emil. "16 Candles." *Vibe*, May 1995. (Retrieved online.) *People* (uncredited.) "Kindred Spirits." *People*. (Retrieved on-line.) Good, Karen R. "Bubbling Brown Sugar." *Vibe*, April 1998. (Retrieved on-line.)

CHAPTER TWO. Raso, Anne M. "Brandy: Live and Let Live!" *The Best of Rap & R&B: Brandy & Monica*, Summer 1998, p. 18-19. Lima, O.J. "Cinderella Has Left the Building." *Seventeen*, September 1998, pp. 258–261. Wilbekin, Emil. "16 Candles." *Vibe*, May 1995. (Retrieved on-line.) Jones IV, James T. "Bubbly Brandy Rises to the Top." *USA Today*, February 14, 1995, p. D-6. Jones, Steve. "At 19, Brandy's Smiling With Success." *USA Today*, June 19, 1998. (Retrieved on-line.) BET Networks chat with Brandy, June 5, 1996. Norment, Lynn. "Brandy." *Ebony*, August 1998, pp. 80–88. *Best of Rap & R&B* (uncredited). "A Quick Q&A With Brandy." *The Best of Rap & R&B: Brandy & Monica*, Summer 1998, p. 20. Raso, Anne M. "Brandy: Live and Let Live!" *The Best of Rap & R&B: Brandy & Monica*, Summer 1998, p. 18–19. Jones, Steve. "At 19, Brandy's Smiling With Success." *USA Today*, June 19, 1998. (Retrieved on-line.) *iMusic* site (uncredited). "Brandy—Biography." (Retrieved on-line.) Helligar, Jeremy. "Starry-Eyed." *People*, 1998. (Retrieved on-line.) Hodges, Ann. "Brandy: Having It All at 16." *Houston Chronicle*, January 25, 1996, p. 5.

CHAPTER THREE. *Best of Rap & R&B* (uncredited). "A Quick Q&A With Brandy." *The Best of Rap & R&B: Brandy & Monica*, Summer 1998, p. 20. Helligar, Jeremy. "Starry-Eyed." *People*, 1998. (Retrieved on-line.) Hodges, Ann. "Brandy: Having It All at 16." *Houston Chronicle*, January 25, 1996, p. 5. BET Networks chat with Brandy, June 5, 1996. Raso, Anne M. "Brandy: Live and Let Live!" *The Best of Rap & R&B: Brandy & Monica*, Summer 1998, p. 18–19. "*Thea*: An Amiable Way to Spend Time." *Los Angeles Times*, September 8, 1993, p. F-12. Rousch, Matt. "Sitcom Stays Safe at Home With *Thea*." *USA Today*, September 8, 1993, p. D-3. Downey, Austin. "Teen Angel." *HX*, July 17, 1998, p. 18-20. Jones IV, James T. "Bubbly Brandy Rises to the Top." *USA Today*, February 14, 1995, p. D-6. *Best of Rap & R&B* (uncredited). "A Quick Q&A With Brandy." *The Best of -Rap & R&B: Brandy & Monica*, Summer 1998, p. 20.

CHAPTER FOUR. Wilbekin, Emil. "16 Candles." *Vibe*, May 1995. (Retrieved on-line.) Hunter, Asondra R. "Brandy . . . Chasing New Challenges." *The Best of Rap & R&B: Brandy & Monica*, Summer 1998, p. 76. Kaplow, Susan. "Brandy." *Seventeen*, April 1995, pp. 158–161. Hampton, Dream. "Brandy." *Vibe*, 1996. (Retrieved on-line.) *CDNow* On-line review (http://www.cdnow.com) Jones IV, James T. "Bubbly Brandy Rises to the Top." *USA Today*, February 14, 1995, p. D-6. Helligar, Jeremy. "Song Brandy." *People*, October 24, 1994. Johnson, Connie. "Record Rack." *Los Angeles Times*, October 30, 1994, p. Calendar-65. Faison, Datu. "Datu Faison's Rhythm Section." *Billboard*, June 6, 1998. (Retrieved on-line.) *Newsweek* (uncredited). "New Faces for the New Year." *Newsweek*, January 9, 1995, p. 56. BET Networks chat with Brandy, June 5, 1996. *Newsweek* (uncredited). "New Faces for the New Year." *Newsweek*, January 9, 1995, p. 56. Kaplow, Susan. "Brandy." *Seventeen*, April 1995, pp. 158–161. Daniels, Karu F. "Too Good To Be True!?" *Mad Rhythms*, September 1998, pp. 28-31. Hodges, Ann. "Brandy: Having It All at 16." *Houston Chronicle*, January 25, 1996, p. 5. Jones IV, James T. "Bubbly Brandy Rises to the Top." *USA Today*, February 14, 1995, p. D-6. Good, Karen R. "Bubbling Brown Sugar." *Vibe*, April 1998. (Retrieved on-line.) Wilbekin, Emil. "16 Candles." *Vibe*, May 1995. (Retrieved on-line.)

CHAPTER FIVE. Marin, Rich and Allison Samuels. "Brandy: Keeping It Real." *Newsweek*, March 25, 1996. Everett, Vic. "Ex-Tomboy Is a Hit in Several Mediums." *Los Angeles Times*, May 21, 1996, p. F-3. Everett, Vic. "Moesha As Social Revolutionary." *Word Up!*, October 1998, p. 37. Marin, Rich and Allison Samuels. "Brandy: Keeping It Real." *Newsweek*, March 25, 1996. *Jet* (uncredited). "Brandy Leads *Moesha* Cast in Third Season." *Jet*, September 8, 1997. (Retrieved on-line.) Mr. *Showbiz* (uncredited). "Brandy: The Mr. *Showbiz* Interview." (Retrieved on-line.) Marin, Rich and Allison Samuels. "Brandy: Keeping It Real." *Newsweek*, March 25, 1996. Malone, Janice. "A Chat With Moesha's Dad—Actor William Allen Young." *New Pittsburgh Courier*, August 27, 1997. (Retrieved online.) Collier, Aldore. "Babyface." *Ebony*, April 1996, pp. 26-30. *People* (uncredited). "10 Best Dressed." *People*, September 16, 1996, p. 77. *Jet* (uncredited). "Singer Brandy Turns Actress in New TV Series *Moesha*." *Jet*, February 26, 1996. (Retrieved on-line.) *People* (uncredited). "40 Most Fascinating People on TV." *People*, 1996. (Retrieved on-line.) Holsey, Steve. "*Moesha* Co-Star and 19-Year-Old Acting 'Veteran' Never Wants to Be a Diva." *Jacksonville Free-Press*, August 27, 1997. (Retrieved on-line.) Marin, Rich and Allison Samuels. "Brandy: Keeping It Real." *Newsweek*, March 25, 1996. Holland, Ty. "Brandy's Hoop Dreamboat." *TV Guide*, August 30–September 5, 1996. (Retrieved on-line.) Daniels, Karu F. "Too Good To Be True!?" *Mad Rhythms*, September 1998, pp. 28-31. Dickensheets, Scott (compiler). "People in the News." *Las Vegas Sun*, May 24, 1996. (Retrieved on-line.) M., Rudi. "Brandy Comes Clean!" *Black Beat*, September 1998, pp. 32–33, 85.

CHAPTER SIX. *Live! With Regis & Kathie Lee* TV broadcast, June 1988. *People* (uncredited). "Brandy Comes of Age." *People*, July 24, 1997. (Retrieved on-line.) *Teen People* (uncredited). "Star Woes." *Teen People*, September 1998, p. 64. Rogers, Charles. "Is Usher the New Prince of Hip-Hop Soul?" *Black Beat's Ultimate Usher*, Summer 1998, pp. 12–14. Rogers, Charles. "Is Usher the New Prince of Hip-Hop Soul?" *Black Beat's Ultimate Usher*, Summer 1998, pp. 12–14. Keets, Heather S. "Brandy's Magic Hour." *Seventeen*, November 1997, pp. 122–123. *Live! With Regis & Kathie Lee* TV broadcast, June 1988. *Time for Kids* (uncredited). "Spotlight: Brandy Norwood." *Time for Kids*, October 31, 1997. (Retrieved on-line.) Keets, Heather S. "Brandy's Magic Hour." *Seventeen*, November 1997, pp. 122–123. James, Caryn. "TV Weekend: The Glass Slipper Fits with a '90s Conscience." *The New York Times*, October 31, 1997. (Retrieved online.) Norment, Lynn. "Brandy." *Ebony*, August 1998, pp. 80–88.

CHAPTER SEVEN. *USA Today* (uncredited). "Brandy Ages Like Fine Wine on 2nd Release." *USA Today*, June 19, 1998. (Retrieved online.) Hunter, Asondra R. "Brandy . . . Chasing New Challenges." *The Best of Rap & R&B: Brandy & Monica*, Summer 1998, p. 76. Handelman, David. "Mix Master." *New York*, August 17, 1998, pp. 28–35. Samuels, Anita M. "Brandy Returns to Music." *Billboard*, April 25, 1998. (Retrieved on-line.) Marder, Keith. "Brandy Goes to College." *Los Angeles Daily News*, January 16, 1997, p. 4. Jacobanis, Carol. "Young, Focused and Movin' On Up." *EMI Songwriter Spotlight*. (Retrieved on-line.) Chambers, Veronica and Allison Samuels. "Diva Rising: Meet the Other Monica." *Newsweek*, July 27, 1998. (Retrieved on-line.) M., Rudi. "Brandy Comes Clean!" *Black Beat*, September 1998, pp. 32–33, 85. Peters, Jan. "Monica!" *Word Up!*, September 1998, p. 15. Lima, O.J. "Cinderella Has Left the Building." *Seventeen*, September 1998, pp. 258–261. M., Rudi. "Brandy Comes Clean!" *Black Beat*, September 1998, pp. 32–33, 85. *Right On!* (uncredited). "Brandy and Mase: The Secret They're Not Trying to Hide." *Right On!*, October 1998, p. 30. Samuels, Anita M. "Brandy Returns to Music." *Billboard*, April 25, 1998. (Retrieved on-line.) *USA Today* (uncredited). "Brandy Ages Like Fine Wine on 2nd Release." *USA Today*, June 19, 1998. (Retrieved on-line.) *Billboard Online* (uncredited). "Brandy *Never Say Never*." *Billboard*, June 13, 1998. Considine, J.D. "Music Reviews: Brandy/*Never Say Never*." *Entertainment Weekly*, June 8, 1998. (Retrieved on-line.) Mills, Nancy. "Field of Scream." *New York Daily News*, September 7, 1998, pp. 31-32. Hunter, Asondra R. "Brandy . . . Chasing New Challenges." *The Best of Rap & R&B: Brandy & Monica*, Summer 1998, p. 76. *Entertainment Weekly* (uncredited). "Fall Movie Preview—*I Still Know What You Did Last Summer*." *Entertainment Weekly*, August 21, 1998. (Retrieved on-line.) *Premiere* (uncredited). "There Goes the Neighborhood." *I Still Know What You Did Last Summer*. *Premiere*, September 1998, p. 68. Beck, Marilyn and Stacy Jenel Smith. "Brandy, Star of Stage and Scream." Syndicated column, 1998. (Retrieved on-line.) Mills, Nancy. "Field of Scream." *New York Daily News*, September 7, 1998, pp. 31-32.

THE BRANDY LOOK. Kaplow, Susan. "Brandy." *Seventeen*, April 1995, p. 158–161. *Teen People* (uncredited). "Hot Stuff: Hair." *Teen People*, September 1998, p. 194. *People* (uncredited). "10 Best Dressed." *People*, September 14, 1998, pp. 110–111.

BRANDY'S MEN. Norment, Lynn. "Brandy." *Ebony*, August 1998, pp. 80–88. Lima, O.J. "Cinderella Has Left the Building." *Seventeen*, September 1998, pp. 258–261. *People* (uncredited). "Kindred Spirits." *People*. (Retrieved on-line.) Rogers, Charles. "Is Usher the New Prince of Hip-Hop Soul?" *Black Beat's Ultimate Usher*, Summer 1998, pp. 12–14.

BRANDY TV/FILM CREDITS. Downey, Austin. "Teen Angel." *HX*, July 17, 1998, pp. 18-20. Wolf, Alissa. "The Singing Sensation Sets Her Sights on Television and Movies." *The Best of Rap & R&B: Brandy & Monica*, Summer 1998, p. 17. *People* (uncredited). "40 Most Fascinating People on TV." *People*, 1996. (Retrieved on-line.) James, Caryn. "TV Weekend: The Glass Slipper Fits with a '90s Conscience." *The New York Times*, October 31, 1997. (Retrieved on-line.)

OTHER REFERENCES: ARTICLES. Arista Records (uncredited). "Monica—Biography." (Retrieved on-line.) Associated Press. "Garth Brooks, Eagles Win Big at American Music Awards Event." *Los Angeles Times*, January 30, 1996, p. B-3. Associated Press. "Tupac Shakur Joins Brotherhood Crusade." *Los Angeles Times*, August 16, 1996. (Retrieved on-line.) *Billboard* (uncredited). "Brandy Sweeps *Soul Train* Awards." *Billboard*, August 19, 1995. (Retrieved on-line.) Bornfeld, Steve. "Dial File: Black and White Isn't Black and White Anymore." *Las Vegas Sun*, June 18, 1998. (Retrieved on-line.) Borzillo, Carrie. "Brandy Bows at No. 3 on the Billboard 200." *Allstar News*, June 17, 1998. (Retrieved on-line.) Bowen, Eugene. "'Immature' Band Members Grow Up Quickly." *The Michigan Daily*, 1996. (Retrieved on-line.) Bronson, Fred. "The Year in Charts." *Billboard*, 1995. (Retrieved on-line.) CelebSite (uncredited). "Brandy—Star Bio." (Retrieved on-line.) Cerone, Daniel Howard. "New Year Brings 2 New Networks." *Los Angeles Times*, January 2, 1995, p. F-1. Chappell, Kevin. "Usher! Backstage with the Hottest Teenager in Music." *Ebony*, August 1998, pp. 118–122. Disney Channel Homepage (uncredited). "Brandy, the Singer." (Retrieved on-line.) Disney Channel Homepage (uncredited). "On the Inside With Ray J." (Retrieved on-line.) DuBrow, Rick. "ABC Thinks 7 Will Be Fall's Lucky Number." *Los Angeles Times*, May 10, 1994, p. F-1. E! Online (uncredited). "Fact Sheet—Brandy." (Retrieved on-line.) *Ebony* (uncredited). "10 Hottest Couples." *Ebony*, February 1998, p. 73. Ehrlich, Dimitri. "Rhythm-and-Blues,

But Not Too Blue." *The New York Times*, June 28, 1998. (Retrieved on-line.) Elliott, Helene. "Ahead of the Class; Kobe Bryant Humbly Begins His Jump from Preps to Pros." *Los Angeles Times*, October 15, 1996, p. C-1. *Entertainment Weekly Online* (uncredited). "Teen Idols." (Retrieved on-line.) Ewey, Melissa. "Miss Thang Grows Up." *Ebony*, September 1998. (Retrieved on-line.) Graham, Jefferson. "TV . . . With Children: Next Fall, Every Night Is Family Night." *USA Today*, May 24, 1993, p. D-1. Helligar, Jeremy. "Upswing." *People*, 1998. (Retrieved on-line.) Hodges, Ann. "*Thea*'s Happy Family." *Houston Chronicle*, September 8, 1993, p. 8. Horovitz, Bruce. "More Advertisers Are Tailoring TV Spots to Ethnicity of Viewers." *Los Angeles Times*, May 3, 1994, p. D-1. *iMusic* site (uncredited). "Mase—Biography." (Retrieved on-line.) Johnson, Richard with Jeane MacIntosh and Kate Coyne. "Dueling Divas in MTV Slap Fight." *New York Post*, September 13, 1998, p. 16. *Los Angeles Times* (uncredited). "Music Fans, Get Out Your Pens." *Los Angeles Times*, February 25, 1996, p. F-9. *Los Angeles Times* (uncredited). Photo caption (Arsenio Hall at Walter Bremond Pioneer of Black Achievement Award event). December 13, 1990. (Retrieved on-line.) M., Rudi. "The Usher One-on-One." *Black Beat's Ultimate Usher*, Summer 1998, pp. 8–10. McWilliams, Michael. "*Moesha* Is a '90s Gidget Morphed With Ricki Lake." *The Detroit News*, January 23, 1996. (Retrieved on-line.) Millner, Denene. "Flying Solo." *Vibe*, June/July 1998. (Retrieved on-line.) National Basketball Association Website (uncredited). "Kobe Bryant—Background." Patrick, Tony. "Brandy/Monica: Sharing Similarities and Success." *The Best of Rap & R&B: Brandy & Monica*, Summer 1998, pp. 10–11. Peters, Jan. "Still a Singer! Brandy's World." *Word Up!*, October 1998, pp. 36–37. Reynolds, J.R. "Arista Acts Top Lady of Soul Awards: Women Honored in Nine Music Categories." *Billboard*, September 21, 1996. (Retrieved on-line.) Reynolds, J.R. "The Rhythm & the Blues." *Billboard*, November 30, 1996. (Retrieved on-line.) *Right On!* (uncredited). "Usher: He's Bold and Beautiful." *Right On!*, October 1998, p. 24. *Rolling Stone* Network Website (uncredited). "Brandy Biography." (Retrieved on-line.) *Rolling Stone* Network Website (uncredited). "Mase Biography." (Retrieved on-line.) Rosenberg, Howard. "Don't Blame Fox TV for Trying to Reach Out." *Los Angeles Times*, October 17, 1994, p. F-1. Rousch, Matt. "A 'Hollywood' Reality Check." *USA Today*, August 3, 1995, p. D-3. Sands, Rich. "The Boys Are Hers." *TV Guide*, July 18–24, 1998. (Retrieved on-line.) Sony Pictures Website. *I Still Know What You Did Last Summer—Official Site*. (Retrieved on-line.) Spaulding, Melinda. "Brandy for Two." *Entertainment Weekly Online*, March 15, 1998. (Retrieved on-line.) Stackhouse, Ray. "The Week's Best Bets for Kids." *TV Guide*, September 20–26, 1997. (Retrieved on-line.) Stein, Joel. "People." *Time*, February 23, 1998. (Retrieved on-line.) Taraska, Julie (editor). "Brandy's Manager Mom Goes Into Production." *Billboard Online*, June 17, 1998. (Retrieved on-line.) *Teen People* (uncredited). "Cliff-hanger Clues." *Teen People*, September 1998. *Ultimate TV* Website. "Who's Hot? Brandy Norwood." (Retrieved on-line.) *Ultimate Usher* (uncredited). "Usher on Girls, Girls—and More Girls!" *Black Beat's Ultimate Usher*, Summer 1998, pp. 66, 77. *USA Today* (uncredited). "Nominees for Soul Train Awards." *USA Today*, August 3, 1995. (Retrieved on-line.) *USA Today* (uncredited). "Winners of the 27th Annual NAACP Image Awards." *USA Today*. (Retrieved on-line.) *Vibe* (uncredited). "About Brandy." *Vibe*, 1996. (Retrieved on-line.) *Wall of Sound* (uncredited). "Boyz II Men Biography." *Wall of Sound* (http://www.wallofsound.com/artists/boyziimen/home.html) Weeks, Janet. "Brandy's Big Moment." *TV Guide*, July 18-24, 1998. (Retrieved on-line.) Westbrook, Bruce. "*Thea* Offers Both Love and Laughter." *Houston Chronicle*, September 8, 1993, p. 1. *Word Up!* (uncredited). "Brandy & Li'l Kim: Model Artists." *Word Up!*, September 1998, p. 57. *Word Up!* (uncredited). "Usher: He's Got The Look." *Word Up!*, September 1998, p. 19. Zaslow, Jeffrey. "Straight Talk: Usher." *USA Weekend*, August 7-9, 1998, p. 15.

BOOKS. Bronson, Fred. *The Billboard Book of Number One Hits*. New York: Billboard Publications, 1988. Farnighetti, Robert. *The World Almanac and Book of Facts*. New Jersey: Funk & Wangalls Corp., 1994. Maltin, Leonard (editor). *Leonard Maltin's 1997 Movie & Video Guide*. New York: Penguin Books, 1996. McNeil, Alex. *Total Television*. New York: Penguin Books, 1996.

WEBSITES. *Billboard Online* (http://www.billboard.com) Singles chart information. *CD Now* (http://www.cdnow.com) Discography information for Aaliyah, Brandy, Tevin Campbell, Kris Kross, Whitney Houston, Immature, Monica, Mase, Puff Daddy, Ray J, Usher. *Celebsite* (http://www.celebsite.com) *City of Carson* (http://www.gjw.com/Fans/Brandy.html) Demographic information about city; biography information about Brandy. *CNN/SI* (http://www.cnnsi.com) Kobe Bryant stats. *Disney Channel* (http://www.disney.com/disneychannel/) *Internet Movie Database* (http://www.imdb.com) Filmography information for William Allen Young, Brandy, Ralph Farquhar, Mekhi Phifer, Sheryl Lee Ralph, Usher, and Countess Vaughn. Credits information for *Moesha*, *Thea*, *I Know What You Did Last Summer*, and *I Still Know What You Did Last Summer*. *iMusic* (http://www.imusic.com) *I Still Know What You Did Last Summer* Official Site (http://www.isstillknow.com) *E! Online* (http://www.eonline.com) *Mr. Showbiz!* (http://www.mrshowbiz.com) *National Basketball Association* (http://www.nba.com) *Pathfinder* (http://www.pathfinder.com) *Pike County, Mississippi* (http://www.telapex.com/~pcedd/info.html#church) Demographic information about McComb, Mississippi. *Rolling Stone Network* (http://www.rollingstone.com) *S.O.U.L. S.Y.S.T.E.M.* (http://www.galactica.it/101/black/) Producer credits for Keith Crouch, Kipper Jones. *Thea* Episode Guide (http://www.avimall.com/entertain/thea.txt) *UPN* (http://www.upn.com/schedule_98/about_moesha.html) *Moesha* credits.